**Monika Ahlberg · Ewa-Marie Rundquist · Kent Nyberg**

# The Garden Café at
# Rosendal

TRANSLATION BY MARTIN HEAP

PRISMA

# Weights and Measures

**WEIGHTS**

| METRIC | IMPERIAL |
|---|---|
| 25 g | 1 oz |
| 50 g | 1 3/4 oz |
| 75 g | 2 1/2 oz |
| 100 g | 3 1/2 oz |
| 125 g | 4 1/2 oz |
| 150 g | 5 1/2 oz |
| 175 g | 6 1/2 oz |
| 200 g | 7 oz |
| 225 g | 8 oz |
| 250 g | 8 1/2 oz |
| 300 g | 10 1/2 oz |
| 400 g | 14 oz |
| 450 g | 16 oz (1 lb) |
| 500 g | 1 lb 2 oz |
| 600 g | 1 lb 6 oz |
| 700 g | 1 lb 9 oz |
| 800 g | 1 lb 12 oz |
| 900 g | 2 lb |
| 1 kg | 2 lb 4 oz |
| 2 kg | 4 lb 8 oz |
| 3 kg | 6 lb 8 oz |
| 4 kg | 9 lb |
| 5 kg | 11 lb |

**VOLUME**

| METRIC | IMPERIAL | AMERICAN |
|---|---|---|
| 50 ml | 2 fl oz | 1/4 cup |
| 75 ml | 3 fl oz | 1/2 cup |
| 1 dl | 4 fl oz | (1/4 pint) |
| 1 1/4 dl | 4 1/2 fl oz | 2/3 cup |
| 1 1/2 dl | 5 fl oz | 3/4 cup |
| 1 2/3 dl | 5 1/2 fl oz | – |
| 1 3/4 dl | 6 fl oz | 3/4 cup |
| 2 dl | 7 fl oz | – |
| 2 1/4 dl | 7 1/2 fl oz | – |
| 2 1/2 dl | 8 fl oz | 1 cup (1/2 pint) |
| 3 dl | 10 fl oz | 1 1/4 cups |
| 3 1/2 dl | 12 fl oz | 1 1/2 cups |
| 4 dl | 14 fl oz | 1 3/4 cups |
| 5 dl | 16 fl oz | 2 cups (1 pint) |
| 6 dl | 21 fl oz | 2 3/4 cups |
| 7 dl | 25 fl oz | 3 cups |
| 8 dl | 28 fl oz | 3 2/3 cups |
| 9 dl | 32 fl oz | 4 cups |
| 1 litre | 35 fl oz | 4 1/2 cups |
| 1 1/2 litres | 50 fl oz | 6 1/4 cups |
| 2 litres | 72 fl oz | 9 cups |

**LENGTH**

| METRIC | IMPERIAL |
|---|---|
| 1 cm | 1/2 in |
| 2 cm | 3/4 in |
| 3 cm | 1 1/4 in |
| 5 cm | 2 in |
| 8 cm | 3 1/4 in |
| 10 cm | 4 in |
| 20 cm | 8 in |
| 23 cm | 9 in |
| 30 cm | 12 in (1 ft) |

**TEMPERATURE**

| CELSIUS | FAHRENHEIT | GAS MARK |
|---|---|---|
| 75 | 165 | – |
| 100 | 212 | 1/4 |
| 150 | 300 | 2 |
| 175 | 335 | 3 |
| 180 | 350 | 4 |
| 200 | 400 | 6 |
| 225 | 435 | 7 |
| 250 | 475 | 9 |
| 275 | 515 | 10 |

Bokförlaget Prisma
Visiting adress: Tryckerigatan 4
P.O. Box 2052, 103 12 Stockholm
E-mail: prisma@prismabok.se
www.prismabok.se

Bokförlaget Prisma is part of
P.A. Norstedts & Söner AB,
founded in 1823

Copyright ©1994:
Copyright holders and Bokförlaget Prisma
through Monika Ahlberg
Text, recipes, idea: Monika Ahlberg
Photography: Ewa-Marie Rundquist
Graphic design: Kent Nyberg

ISBN 91-518-3936-9

# Contents

# It all depends on the person

*by*
*Lars Krantz, master gardener*

Why do some things in this world concern me more than others? They appeal, attract and touch. It is seldom anything run-of-the-mill. No, they have their own special, unique and personal language. A language I recognise and which is addressed to me alone. Sometimes they seem always to have been a part of my life and always will be. Often, of course, they are things that come from my own hands and are therefore particularly dear to me. Or at least they have been created in a way that I can easily and clearly understand. They are like signed originals and acquire a life of their own. Life that gets nourishment from the same context that I am a part of.

I have noticed that even cakes can have a life of their own! Now, I must admit, I do not bake myself. I can't even trust my own judgement to decide whether a cake is good or not. Yet I know for certain whether it appeals to me. The flavour of a cake goes far beyond its potential ability to please my taste buds. What I value has also to do with how the cake came into being, its biography. A context that I also wish to sense and taste! I want to experience how the ingredients have been prepared by the earth that gets the seeds, berries and fruit to swell and how the sun brings forth the sweetness and aroma of the crops. To see the people that harvest, compose and bake using the raw ingredients that have been carried across the threshold of the kitchen and bakery. To smell the scents and feel the heat of the oven as it transforms pale doughs into golden pastries. That is presumably why I have such respect for HOME-BAKED and the reason why I literally love Rosendal's cakes.

Even at the beginning there was a seed, a dream, a vision of a home bakery as a part of the garden. The first attempts came into being with small, small steps. A coffee-pot was placed in the shop and a few lemon cakes were made with the help of friends and acquaintances.

There weren't many guests and the cakes were often divided up among the grateful workers at the end of the day. Pål Borg prepared the ground for the succeeding cake feasts, later on with Gittan Rothkopf. The cucumbers in one of the glasshouses were ousted to make room for a café that began to take shape. The queues to the cake-tables grew and they really had to work to refill the empty plates. But nothing lasts forever and one day Pål and Gittan decided to grow in another direction. Alas, how would things work out? After all, it depends on the people, the enthusiasts, if an initiative is to bear fruit or not. And now there was no one to feed the bakery oven.

Or was there someone? Destiny wove its web and suddenly a certain Monika Ahlberg stood there, whose chief merit in this context was that her grandfather had been a baker. There was no denying that she loved all the good things that life had to offer. Including cakes, but would that really be enough? She had already helped out occasionally with baking and serving when not occupied by dancing, which was her real profession. But she was hardly the classic type of baker who rises before the sun each morning. On the contrary she appeared more to be a queen of the night who crawled to bed after the sun had gone up again. But there was this thing about enthusiasm. To love your work and believe in your capabilities. In spite of the amateurism, it was that warm commitment that gave Monika a competence over and above the ordinary. With her heart beating for everything she became involved in, we too wanted to believe with Monika in a continued development of the café after all.

"My God, we will have to learn as we go along". Thus our kitchen became for a while a workshop where experimentation, research and tasting came to characterise our work. When I come to think of it, I think that it is still that searching spirit, that will to learn, to deepen and to go further that is the driving force behind Monika's creativity. At best this means that the guests' reward is not just newly baked bread to enjoy but also new, fresh ideas to take home. Ideas and impulses to inspire their own creativity at the baking table.

If the baker, like Monika, puts a large part of her soul

into her work, then it is an exciting moment when the results meet customers. There is trepidation in the air, but also satisfaction, when she can directly read the expressions of the cake-eating guests. Are they nodding in pleasure or possibly even shaking their heads? Well, everything can't please everybody, but it is nonetheless satisfying when those real gourmets and cake specialists, the choosy children and the equally fastidious old ladies, can be seen munching on the same cakes week in and week out. The very thought of their favourite cake being off for the day would be a catastrophe.

As an uninitiated, I cannot help but be astonished by the fact that something we put in our mouths can give rise to so many lively conversations. Stimulated by their culinary impressions the guests, between chews, discuss recipes, ingredients, fermentation, baking times and much more. With such fascination and involvement that I start to see that not just the baking, but also the tasting, is a great art. An art that looks as if it ought to enrich the lives of most people. I shall just have to start practising and look forward to discovering new worlds together with Monika and her book.

As to the question of how things would turn out with a dancer instead of a baker in the café, even if there were people like me who had certain doubts, I can just say that: it works, and how! I say it again; it all depends on the person!

Our guests often ask me which cake is the best, but I can never answer. It would be like saying which flower is the most beautiful or which love is the greatest.

All my cakes are good! Each in its own way. One is good because of the way it looks, another for its character and charm. Another one is good because of its wonderful smell and yet another because it melts in the mouth and works wonders in the stomach.

One thing, however, is certain: I try to serve only such cakes, pastries, sandwiches and dishes that have something of rustic nobility about them, and as far as possible have some ingredient from our own garden.

Meny 3

Fårostsallad

Matjessill, grä"
gräslök skalpotatis

Italiensk ta"

Provençalsk 68

Varmrökt lax u basilika
inkl. små bröd Potatis 65

Berries

So pale and colourless they look. So hard and sour they taste! Yes, that's how most of the different kinds of berries seem, when I'm impatiently waiting for them to ripen. But suddenly one morning as I stroll through the allotment there they are: the sun-ripened, sweet, red strawberries. So reverently I taste the first! Mmm, so delicious. Then things happen fast. They rush into my stomach one after the other, and my fingers are stained red.

After a few days, the strawberries are joined by the raspberries, which spread their marvellous scent from the nearby bushes. What can taste better than raspberries eaten directly from the bush? Our supply of strawberries and raspberries at Rosendal is limited. Quite simply because we eat them up ourselves directly as we pick them! On the other hand we've plenty of currants. Abundant bunches of red and black berries. This is when the berry tarts make their entrance at the café. And when the shelves in the shop are filled with jam, jelly, squash and other preservatives.

It seems to be the general opinion these days that making jam, fruit-syrup and preservatives is difficult. But in fact it's easy and fun to see your own berries processed and stored in beautiful jars. Another simple way to extend the summer through to the next, is to create a store of berries in the freezer. Everyone should be granted the luxury of a couple of spoonfuls of raspberries in their breakfast bowl on a dark winter morning!

Jam kisses, jam buns and swiss roll with jam.

## Jam kisses
*(Makes about 30)*

*Small, tasty kisses. They are easy to bake, sweet and dainty, and with raspberry jam in the middle.*

*Tarts:*
200 g butter
1 dl icing sugar
1 dl potato flour
4 dl flour

*For garnishing:*
About 2 dl raspberry jam

• Mix the butter and icing sugar together. Add the flour and potato flour.
• Roll the dough into walnut-size pieces and put them on a greased baking sheet. Make a hole in each ball. Fill each hole with raspberry jam.
• Bake the kisses at 175° for about 10 minutes.

## Swiss roll with jam
*Cake:*
3 eggs
2 dl sugar
2 dl flour
2 tsp baking powder
1/2 dl double cream

*Filling:*
3 dl stirred fresh blackcurrants (or other berries). Sugar according to taste.

• Whisk the egg and sugar white and fluffy.
• Mix the flour and the baking powder. Add this alternately with the cream to the egg and sugar mixture.
• Spread the mixture on to greaseproof paper in a roasting pan.
• Bake at 250° for 5 minutes.
• Sprinkle the cake with sugar. Lay a piece of greaseproof paper on top and turn the cake over onto a baking sheet. Remove the other piece of greaseproof paper.
• Spread the jam over the cake and roll up from the long side. Place with the join underneath. Cut the cake into pieces and serve with whipped cream if desired.

## Blueberry muffins
*(Makes about 20)*

*Muffins made with berries or vegetables are very common in the U.S.A., for example, but not in Sweden. These blueberry muffins are very good and greatly appreciated when we have them at the garden café.*

5 dl flour
2 dl sugar
2 tsp baking powder
1/2 tsp salt
6 dl blueberries
Peel of 2 lemons, grated
2 eggs
2 tbsp crème fraiche
1 dl milk

• Mix together all the dry ingredients with the blueberries in a bowl.
• Add eggs, crème fraiche and milk.
• Stir together carefully until thoroughly mixed. Make sure not to squash the blueberries too much.
• Drop or pipe the mixture into muffin forms. Fill them not more than two thirds full.
• Bake at 180° for 20–25 minutes.

## Jam buns
*(Makes about 10)*

*These big, smooth newly baked buns with a blob of jam in the middle taste best with a glass of milk. Enticing smells, a mixture of buns baking and jam cooking, spreads throughout our garden when we are making jam buns. They are then consumed as soon as they hit the cake-table in the glasshouse.*

*Buns:*
75 g butter
2 1/2 dl milk
25 g fresh yeast
1/2 tsp salt
1/2 dl sugar
2 tsp vanilla sugar
1 small egg
About 7 dl flour

*For the filling:*
About 1 dl raspberry jam

*For glazing:*
1 egg

• Melt the butter and pour in the milk. Heat to lukewarm.
• Dissolve the yeast in the liquid. Add the salt, sugar, vanilla sugar, egg and flour, a little at a time. Save about 1 dl for the second kneading.
• Knead the dough vigorously until it is smooth and elastic and comes away from the bowl. Add more flour if necessary. Cover with a cloth and leave to rise for about 40 minutes.
• Knead the dough and form into buns. Make a hole in each and fill with raspberry jam. Leave to rise on greased baking sheets under cloths for about 15–20 minutes. Glaze the buns with egg.
• Bake at 225° for about 10–15 minutes.

## Raspberry tart

*Actually, I think that raspberries are best eaten straight from the bush. There are sometimes, however, a few left over for this exquisite tart, which is delicious with cream.*

*Pastry:*
150 g butter
3 1/2 dl flour
2 tbsp icing sugar
2 tbsp cold water

*Filling:*
4 egg yolks
2 dl double cream
3 tbsp sugar
1 tbsp vanilla sugar
6 dl raspberries

*Pastry:*
• Mix together the ingredients for the pastry and leave it in a cold place for an hour.
• Roll out the pastry and line a detachable tart ring (about 23 cm in diameter). Prick the pastry with a fork and bake blind at 200° for about 5 minutes.

*Filling:*
• Whisk the egg yolks in one bowl, and the cream in another. Add the sugar and the vanilla sugar to the cream and mix with the egg yolks.
• Pour the filling into the pre-baked and somewhat cooled tart case. Spread the raspberries on top.
• Bake the tart at 180° for about 15 minutes until the filling has set.

## Raspberry and apple tart

*Pastry:*
150 g cold butter
5 tbsp cold water
2 1/2 dl flour
1/2 dl sugar

*Filling:*
4–5 apples
1/2 l raspberries
1 dl flour
1 dl sugar
2 tsp cinnamon

*Topping:*
150 g cold butter
3 tbsp sugar
2 1/4 dl demerara sugar
2 tsp cinnamon

*Pastry:*
• Mix together all the ingredients for the pastry in a mixer or by hand. Press out the pastry into a tart ring (about 23 cm in diameter). Prick the bottom with a fork and cover the edge with foil.
• Bake blind at 200° for 10 minutes.

*Filling:*
• Core the apples and slice thinly (peel if necessary).
• Mix all the ingredients for the filling in a bowl. Then fill the pre-baked tart case with the mixture.

*Topping:*
• Mix all the ingredients together, using a mixer if you wish, and spread out the topping over the filling.
• Bake the tart at 180° for about 30 minutes. Serve with whipped cream.

## Strawberry tart with elderberry and lemon balm

*It was perhaps this very strawberry tart that inspired Sven-Bertil's essay on strawberries, Indians and other things. With flavours such as strawberry, elderberry and lemon balm it is easy for your thoughts to take wing. One person might remember a strawberry patch, another an elderberry tree or a herb garden.*

*Pastry:*
100 g butter
3 dl flour
150 g almond paste
1 tbsp water

*Filling:*
3 egg yokes
1 dl sugar
1/2–1 dl undiluted elderberry juice
Peel of 1 orange, grated

*Decoration:*
1 l strawberries
Leaves of lemon balm

*Pastry:*
• Chop the butter, flour and almond paste together in a mixer or with a knife
• Add water and quickly bind the mixture. Leave in a cool place for about 20 minutes.
• Press out the dough into a detachable tart ring (about 23 cm in diameter).
• Bake blind at 200° for 15 minutes. Then reduce the heat to 175°.

*(Continued on page 26)*

Raspberry and apple tart, blueberry muffins and raspberry tart. *Previous spread*: strawberry cake with elderberry and lemon balm.

Lingonberry tart with stirred lingonberry compote. *Next page:* Blueberry soufflé.

*Filling:*
• Whisk together egg yolks and sugar until fluffy.
• Add the elderberry juice and the grated orange peel. Pour the filling into the pre-baked tart case.
• Bake for 15–20 minutes until golden.
• Decorate with the strawberries and the lemon balm leaves. Serve with lightly whipped cream.

## Red currant tart with meringue topping

*Pastry:*
3 1/2 dl flour
4 tbsp icing sugar
150 g butter
1 large egg yolk
1 tbsp water

*Filling:*
About 1 l red currants
3–5 tbsp sugar
1 tsp potato flour

*Meringue:*
3 egg whites
2 dl sugar

*Pastry:*
• Mix together the flour and icing sugar and rub in the fat. Use a mixer if you prefer. Add the egg yolk and water and work into supple pastry.
• Roll out the pastry and line a detachable tart ring (about 23 cm in diameter). Cover the edge with foil. Place in a cool place for about 30 minutes.
• Bake blind at 200° for about 15–20 minutes.

*Filling and meringue:*
• Rinse and clean the red currants. Mix them with sugar and potato flour.
• Whisk the egg whites until stiff and stir in the sugar.
• Spread the red currants over the tart base and cover them with the meringue.
• Bake the tart at 200° for about 15 minutes or until the meringue is pale golden.

## Lingonberry or cranberry tart

*Lingonberries aren't the kind of berries you usually use in baking. This is a pity, I think, because lingonberries give a fine, tangy flavour. If you can't get lingonberries, use cranberries instead. Whipped cream is delicious with this pie.*

*Pastry:*
3 1/2 dl flour
1/2 dl sugar
150 g butter
2 egg yolks
2 tbsp cream or water

*Filling:*
2 1/2 dl fresh lingonberries or cranberries, stirred
80 g butter
2 1/2 dl porridge oats (oat meal)
1 1/2 dl sugar

*Pastry:*
• Mix together the flour and the sugar. Rub in the butter until the mixture has a grainy texture. Add the egg yolks and cream, and lightly work together into a supple pastry.
• Roll out the pastry and line a detachable tart ring (about 23 cm in diameter). Cover the edge with foil. Place in a cold place for about 30 minutes.
• Bake blind at 200° for 10 minutes.

*Filling:*
• Spread the lingonberry jam over the tart base.
• Melt the butter and pour over the oats. Let the mixture stand for a few minutes. Mix in the sugar and spread the mixture over the lingonberry jam.
• Bake the tart at 180° for about 25 minutes.

## Blackcurrant cake with almonds

*Cake:*
5 eggs
3 dl sugar
150 g grated almond paste
About 4 dl flour
1 dl pearl sugar
75 g butter

*Filling:*
About 8 dl blackcurrants.

• Whisk the egg and sugar until white and fluffy.
• Coarsely grate the almond paste and add to the mixture. Stir in the flour and mix well.
• Rinse and clean the blackcurrants.
• Spread out the cake mixture on to a greased and breadcrumbed baking tin (about 23 cm in diameter).
• Spread the blackcurrants over the mixture and press down. Sprinkle the cake with pearl sugar. Use a cheese slicer to make thin slices of butter and cover the cake with them.
• Bake the cake at about 200° for 45 minutes. Serve with Rosendal's custard if you like.

# My favourite berry dessert
*(For 4–5 servings)*

*A wonderful dessert that is easy to make even for a larger number of guests. When we have a buffet in the garden café I sometimes serve this very dessert. I make it in large, beautiful ovenproof dishes and serve it with almond or oat wafers and whipped cream. Decorate with lots of lemon balm leaves.*

1 l raspberries
8 egg yolks
About 1/2 dl sugar and 1/2 vanilla pod or 1/2 dl Rosendal's vanilla sugar
1 dl double cream
1 dl white wine

*For decoration:*
Lemon balm leaves

• Make sure all the ingredients are at room temperature.
• Spread out the raspberries in an ovenproof dish.
• Whisk the egg yolks and the sugar. Whisk the cream and mix with the wine and the vanilla seeds.
• Mix the cream mixture into the egg mixture and spread over the raspberries.
• Bake at 180° for about 15 minutes. Dot the dessert with small scoops of full-cream ice and decorate with leaves of lemon balm. Serve immediately.

# Blueberry soufflé
*(For 4 servings)*

*Don't be afraid to try this soufflé. It's so easy to make, you can't fail.*

1 dl sugar
6 egg whites
1 wedge of lemon
2 dl fresh blueberries
3 tbsp water

*For decoration:*
Icing sugar

• Grease a soufflé dish (with room for about a litre). Sprinkle with sugar.
• Whisk the egg whites until stiff in a fat-free bowl that has been rubbed with a wedge of lemon.
• Mix the sugar into the whisked egg whites.
• Crush the blueberries with a fork, together with the water. Mix carefully into the whisked egg whites.
• Bake at 200° for 10–15 minutes at the bottom of the oven.
• Powder with a little icing sugar and serve immediately, with a little whipped cream or full-cream ice.

# Raspberry sauce
*(About 5 servings)*

*This sauce is delicious with ice cream. It goes beautifully with dark chocolate cake and tastes scrumptious with our white chocolate mousse cake.*

1–2 dl cream
250 g frozen raspberries
Sugar to taste

• Whisk the cream. Put the raspberries in a mixer and add the cream, a little at a time, until the mixture has a smooth consistency. Add sugar to taste.

# Strawberry and rhubarb fruit-syrup
*(About 2 litres)*

*A wonderful early summer fruit-syrup that is easy to make.*

1 l strawberries
1 kg rhubarb
8 dl water
6 dl sugar to each litre fruit juice

• Rinse the rhubarb and peel if necessary. (Small tender rhubarb stalks with thin skin do not need to be peeled.) Chop into pieces. Tail the strawberries.
• Boil the water. Put in the rhubarb and strawberries and boil for 10–15 minutes. The rhubarb should be soft and the strawberries colourless. Stir occasionally.
• Pour into a muslin bag and leave to strain for 30–40 minutes.
• Measure the juice and add the correct amount of sugar. Bring to the boil and let boil for 5–10 minutes. Remove from the heat and skim well.
• Pour the fruit syrup into hot, well-cleaned bottles. For the fruit syrup to keep best, fill right up to the neck. Seal immediately with well-cleaned screw-caps or boiled corks. Store in a cool place.

# Blackcurrant jam
*(About 1 litre)*

*Recipes for blackcurrant jam can be found in almost every cookbook from the beginning of the last century. This recipe, with small variations, is to be found in many of them.*

2 l blackcurrants
1 dl water
2 l sugar

• Rinse the berries carefully. Clean them and put into a large saucepan and pour on water. Boil slowly under a lid for 10–15 minutes. Skim well and remove any bits.
• Remove from the heat and mix in the sugar. Stir until the sugar has dissolved.
• Pour carefully into hot, well-cleaned jars and cover immediately. Store in a cool place.

Strawberry jam, raspberry jam and plum jam with walnuts & vanilla.

## RUM JAR

*Who doesn't want to prolong the enjoyment of summer berries? A classic, proven method is the rum jar. The berries must be of the best quality, preferably freshly picked. They should be cleaned but not rinsed.*

Mixed berries
Equal amounts of sugar and berries
White rum
One large or two smaller jars

• Alternate layers of berries and sugar in well-cleaned jars. Stir carefully. Pour rum over the berries until they are covered.
• Seal well. Leave to mature in a cool, dark place for 2–3 months until the berries are ready to be enjoyed.
• You can add berries according to season. Always add the same amount of sugar as berries and pour over more rum, if necessary, to cover the fruit.
• The berries taste divine with lightly whipped cream or full-cream ice. They can also be used as a filling for a cake or tart.

# Lingonberry compote
*(About 1 1/4 litres)*

1 1/2 l lingonberries or cranberries
9 dl sugar

• Briskly mix the berries with the sugar, until the sugar has dissolved. Make sure not to crush the berries too much.
• Keep the conserve in the fridge in a well-cleaned container. If you make a larger amount you can freeze them in smaller plastic boxes.

# Raspberry jam
*(About 1 litre)*

*Second only to rose leaf jam, this is probably the most beautiful jam. The smell of the boiling raspberries is heavenly.*

2 l raspberries
1 large lemon
1 l sugar

• Pick over the raspberries and put them in a large pot. Clean the lemon carefully. Grate the peel and squeeze out the juice. Add this to the raspberries.
• Bring to the boil and then simmer for about ten minutes. Shake the pot occasionally.
• Carefully mix in the sugar and allow to boil without a lid for about 15–25 minutes until the jam has thickened. Stir the berries now and then with a wooden spoon. Test the jam (see page 214).
• Scoop the jam into hot, well-cleaned jars and seal immediately. Store in a cool place.

# Strawberry jam
*Whole strawberries shine like jewels in this delicious jam.*

2 l strawberries
1 3/4 l sugar
Juice and peel of 1 orange
Juice and peel of 1 lemon

• Mix all the ingredients in a large pot and bring slowly to the boil. Stir carefully now and then.
• Let the jam simmer for 10–20 minutes. Shake the pot a few times.
• Remove from the heat and leave the jam for a few minutes. Skim off the froth.
• Scoop into hot, well-cleaned jars and seal immediately. Store in a cool place.

# Raspberry and red currant jam
*(Makes about 1 1/2 litres)*

*Raspberries and red currants are a brilliant combination. The flavour is exquisite, and the different reds of the berries look wonderful.*

1 1/2 l red currants
1 1/4 dl water
Juice and peel of 1 lemon
1 1/2 l raspberries
9 dl sugar

• Pick over the currants and put into the jam-cooking pot. Pour on the water and simmer under a lid for 5–10 minutes, shaking the pot a few times.
• Clean the lemon carefully. Grate the peel and squeeze out the juice. Mix in with the raspberries and the sugar. Boil the jam for a further 15 minutes until the sugar has melted. Stir carefully now and then.
• Scoop into hot, well-cleaned jars and seal immediately. Store in a cool place.

Blackcurrant jam and blackcurrant cake with almond.

*Previous page:* My wedding cakes can look like this! The choice of fruit and berries depends on two things: the wishes of the bridal couple and the season! Lots of couples get married in our garden under their favourite apple tree during the warmer part of the year.

Fredsborg heter stället där jag vistades som barn. Det bebaddes först och främst av min mormor, därefter av tre systrar (hennes) (döttrar). Den äldsta var min mor med man och två barn, min syster Agneta och jag. Fredsborg låg några kilometer från Åkers Runö station på Roslagsbanan.

Det var i början av augusti som korg= makaren kom. Han kom på cykel uppför vägen till mormors hus – den var strödd med kiselsten och röd fältspat – och tog emot hennes beställningar. Och mormor beställde: hon kom från landet, närmare bestämt från (Kalmar) (traktern av), och var van vid kringresande hantverkare. Sedan satte han sig under den stora eken vid grinden, letade i den stora säcken med spån och vidje som han hade på pakethållaren och började fläta de korgar mormor ville ha.

Vi, min kusin Hasse och jag, satte oss i gräset och såg på hur de flinka fingrarna arbetade. På eftermiddagen kom mormor ner med kaffe och smörgåsar åt oss alla tre. Till Fredsborg hörde en stor frukt= trädgård med päron och äpplen, krusbär och jordgubbar. Några dagar efter korgmakarens

besök skördades vinbärsskörden. Det var en
årlig ceremoni som snart följdes av ännu en.
vinbären med kvistar, löv och allt
hälldes i stora, djupa kastruller och
kokades med en skvätt vatten tills de sprack.
Därefter hälldes vinbärsmassan i stora
vita strutar (av tyll?) som bands vid
benen på uppochnedvända stolar. Under
ställdes bunkar som fångade upp den ljuvliga
droppande saften.
Den som varit i ett hus där man
bränner hembränt vet hur det låter.
Jag ser framför mig en dussin vita
strutar och hör det försynta droppandet:
DRIPP DROPP DRIPP DROPP DROPP DROPP

När saften var färdigdroppad bjöds
det på vinbärsfest i bersån och
till den serverades nygräddade bullar
och kakor.
Det var sommar och augusti, kriget       1942)
fortsatte och nätterna blev mörkare
och mörkare.

                              Lars Fresxen

Toppsockret! Jag glömde)
(toppsockret som var saftens sötningsmedel. Finns
de ännu att köpa, dessa kokar av socker som inslagna i grovt
vitt papper vidgades som ananasskivor, större och större ned till foten?

Fruit

There are all kinds of fruit. Round, long, soft, hard, colourful, pale, sweet and sour. Maybe that's why it is so rewarding to mix fruit into cakes, jams, marmalades and more. As they ripen the fruit lead us through the season. Their growth is often expressive and fascinating. The green leaves come first, then the delicate buds develop, followed by a mass of blossom. Finally the individual fruit ripens before it is harvested. We can follow all this in our own garden, although, of course, each fruit develops differently.

A beautifully arranged fruit basket can be just as sensual and colourful as a bouquet of flowers. This isn't so strange if we bear in mind that the simplest of fruits can be cousin to the most exotic berries or the most exclusive flowers. The apple, for example, is related to both wild strawberries and roses. This knowledge makes me happy in a way. Maybe because I'm extremely enchanted with apples, wild strawberries and roses!

There are many sagas and legends that tell us about a miscellany of fruit and their importance for love, knowledge or beauty, wisdom, life or death and, yes, even war.

In Greek mythology there are many legends about the apple, which has probably meant more for us in our time than we suppose. Just think, it was only because Paris, the royal son of Troy, gave the apple of eternal youth to Aphrodite, the goddess of love, who in her turn gave it to Helen, the beautiful queen of Sparta, that Troy and Sparta were at war for an age and the apple of discord was born.

Although, of course, everything had begun much earlier. The queen of the Gods was given an apple tree by Mother Earth because she married Zeus. She planted the tree and it produced the golden fruit that could grant eternal youth and beauty.

The fact that it was the apple that forced Adam and Eve to leave the Garden of Eden is, perhaps, a clear indication of how irresistible or dangerous this fruit can be.

As we know, the apple was also of decisive significance for William Tell. If he hadn't hit the apple he would have hit his own son.

Our apple harvest at Rosendal is not quite so dramatic, but there is a certain drama to the Apple Show that we organise with great delight and energy on the first weekend of October every year.

Our master gardener, Lars Krantz, frequently travels the length and breadth of the country to collect as many varieties as there are of Swedish-grown apples.

He sometimes finds one or two real rarities among the 350 different varieties that can be seen at the Show. They can have such wonderful names as Virginian Rose or Great Transparent Astrakhan. He doesn't have to go too far, however, to fetch one of the most unusual kinds. The original tree grows in our garden here at Rosendal and has the name Södermanland's Kalvill. Grafts have been taken in more recent times and thus it can now be found in a few other places.

One or two apples of each variety are put into small baskets in our largest glasshouse that then serves as the exhibition hall. Occasionally an apple might be a little damaged or has begun to shrivel.

But woe betide him who treats it roughly, this, the beautiful and precious apple!

## Seville orange rusks

*(Makes about 50)*

*A hard and crisp almond rusk with a slight bitter flavour of Seville orange. This rusk contains no fat. The almonds' own oil serves as a binder, with the eggs. It is very common in Italy to dip almond rusks in a glass of sweet white wine, such as Vino Santo. It's well worth a try!*

120 g almonds
2 eggs
2 dl sugar
1/2–1 dl candied orange peel
2–3 tbsp freshly crushed Seville orange peel
1 tsp salt
About 5–6 dl flour
1 tsp baking powder
100 g dark Belgian cooking chocolate, roughly chopped

*To glaze:*
1 egg white

• Grind a third of the almond finely and chop the rest *very* roughly.
• Mix the almond, egg, sugar, orange and Seville orange peel, and salt. Add 3 dl of the flour mixed with the baking powder. Lightly flour the chocolate and add to the mixture. Finally mix in the rest of the flour, a little at a time. Make sure not to add too much.
• Roll out into lengths and place them on greased baking sheets. Brush with the egg white.
• Bake at 180° for about 15–20 minutes.
• Cut the lengths into rusks and dry at 100° for about 30–40 minutes.

## Apple muffins

*(Makes about 20)*

*These muffins are very moist and keep well, thanks to the grated apple in the batter mixture. I flavour them with cardamom and cinnamon, which are well-known apple spices.*

2 dl oil (not olive oil)
3 dl sugar
2 apples
3 eggs
4 dl flour
1 tsp baking powder
1 tsp bicarbonate
1 tbsp cinnamon
1 tbsp freshly crushed cardamom

*Filling:*
3 red apples, not too large
1/2 dl sugar and 1 tsp cinnamon

• Whisk the oil and the sugar vigorously.
• Grate the apples. Add them and the eggs.

• Mix together the flour, baking powder, bicarbonate and the spices. Then stir into the batter.
• Pipe the mixture into muffin cases. Fill them about half full.
• Core and thinly slice the apples. Turn each slice in the cinnamon-and-sugar and press one or two slices into each muffin.
• Bake at 200° for 15–20 minutes.

## Apple croissants

50 g fresh yeast
150 g butter
4 dl milk
6 tbsp sugar
1 egg
1/2 tsp salt
About 1 1/2 l flour

*Filling:*
About 1 1/2 dl mashed apple
2–3 newly crushed cardamoms

*To glaze:*
1 egg

• Melt the butter and pour in the milk. Heat to luke-warm.
• Dissolve the yeast in the liquid. Add sugar, eggs, salt and 1 litre of the flour. Knead the dough until shiny. Use more flour if necessary. Leave the dough to rise under a cloth for about 30 minutes.
• Knead the dough again. Divide into 5–6 pieces. Roll out each piece into a rectangle. Cut out triangles with a pastry cutter or knife.
• Mix the cardamom into the mashed apple. Put a blob onto each triangle. Roll up the croissants from the broad edge to the sharp edge. Put them with the join downwards on greased baking sheets. Leave to rise for 25 minutes. Brush with the egg.
• Bake at 250° for 8–12 minutes.

## Apple burgers

*A very tasty filled bun that came about during our Apple Show, when we had to come up with every imaginable kind of cake and pastry with apples in them. The name is due to the bun being folded more or less like a hamburger.*

25 g fresh yeast
2 1/2 dl milk
100 g butter
1 egg
1/2 tsp salt
1 dl sugar
About 1 l flour

*Filling:*
4 apples
About 150 g butter

5 tbsp sugar
5 tbsp cinnamon

*For glazing:*
Melted butter
Sugar

• Melt the butter and mix into the milk. Heat to luke-warm. Dissolve the yeast in the liquid. Add the lightly whisked egg.
• Mix in the sugar, salt and most of the flour. Knead the dough until it is shiny and supple. Use more flour if necessary. Leave to rise for about 30 minutes.

*Filling:*
• Peel, core and thinly slice the apples. Mix the cinnamon and the sugar. Place the apple slices in a bowl and cover with the sugar-cinnamon mixture.
• Roll out the pastry until it is about 1 1/2 cm thick. Use a glass to cut out circles. Put some slices of apple and a knob of butter on half the circles. Put the empty circles on top and press the edges together.
• Put the "burgers" on a greased baking sheet and leave to rise for about 30 minutes.
• Bake at 250° for 8–10 minutes.
• Brush the "burgers" with the melted butter and turn them in the sugar.

## Rhubarb and nut cake
*(Two baking tins of about 1 1/2 litres each)*

*This is a moist, slightly sour cake made from rhubarb, that wonderful augury of spring. As soon as they appear I put the first stalks of rhubarb into cakes and tarts. This particular cake has a beautiful combination of a darker surface broken up with light pink pieces of rhubarb.*

3–4 dl rhubarb, cut into small pieces
50 g walnuts
50 g hazelnuts
2 1/2 dl brown sugar
1 1/2 dl sunflower oil
1 egg
2 dl sour cream
1 tsp bicarbonate
1 tsp baking powder
1 tsp salt
1 tbsp vanilla sugar
5 dl flour

• Clean the rhubarb. Cut into small pieces. Chop the nuts quite finely.
• Whisk the oil and the brown sugar. Add the egg.
• Mix the flour, bicarbonate, baking powder, salt and vanilla sugar. Add to the mixture alternately with the sour cream. Finally mix in the nuts and the pieces of rhubarb. Pour the mixture into greased and bread-crumbed cake tins.
• Bake the cakes at 175° for about 45 minutes.

## Rhubarb tart
*Pastry:*
200 g butter
4 dl flour
1 tbsp vanilla sugar
2 tbsp water
2 tbsp double cream

*Filling:*
400 g rhubarb
100 g almond paste
Peel and juice from 1 lemon
50 g butter
2 eggs
1 egg white
1 dl sugar

*Pastry:*
• Mix together all the pastry ingredients and work into a dough. Chill for about an hour.
• Roll out about 2/3 of the pastry and put in a tart ring (about 23 cm in diameter). Prick the bottom with a fork and cover the edges with aluminium foil.
• Bake blind at 200° for 5 minutes.

*Filling:*
• Peel and chop the rhubarb into smallish pieces. Grate the almond paste and the lemon peel. Squeeze the juice out of the lemon.
• Melt the butter in a pan. Whisk the egg, sugar and egg yolk in a bowl and add the mixture to the melted butter. Simmer for a few minutes. Remove from the heat and mix in the almond paste and the lemon. Stir into a smooth mixture.
• Fill the pre-baked tart case with the rhubarb, then pour the filling over.
• Roll out the rest of the pastry and cut out strips. Use these to make a lattice top.
• Bake the tart at 180° for about 15–20 minutes. Serve with whipped cream.

Rhubarb compote with whipped cream, strawberry and rhubarb juice, rhubarb and almond cake, rhubarb tart, rhubarb and nut cake and rhubarb jam. In the background strawberry vinegar and rhubarb vinegar.

## Rhubarb cake with almond

*A large, generous and very easy-to-bake cake. The almond flavour combines well with the sharp taste of the rhubarb. We serve it with our home-made vanilla custard.*

500 g rhubarb
5 eggs
3 dl sugar
Almost 4 dl flour
150 g almond paste
1 dl pearl sugar
75 g butter

• Clean and cut the rhubarb into small pieces.
• Whisk the egg and sugar until white and fluffy. Grate the almond paste and fold into the mixture with the flour.
• Pour into a greased and breadcrumbed cake tin (about 23 cm in diameter). Press down and spread the pieces of rhubarb over the mixture. Sprinkle over the pearl sugar and cover with thin slices of butter.
• Bake at 175° for 30–40 minutes.

## Plum cake

*Red, blue or yellow, plums are sweet and juicy. We usually have a good harvest, so there's enough for baking, jam-making and perhaps even chutney. This is the recipe for a beautiful and smooth plum cake that we serve with whipped cream.*

*Cake:*
75 g butter
1 dl sugar
1 tbsp vanilla sugar
2 eggs
Scant 2 dl flour
1 tsp baking powder
About 12–15 plums, fairly large

*Filling:*
1/2 dl sugar
1 dl double cream
1 egg
1/2–1 dl hazelnuts
Grated peel of 1/2 lemon

*Cake:*
• Mix the butter, sugar and vanilla sugar until white and fluffy. Add the eggs and finally the flour mixed with baking powder.
• Pour into a greased and breadcrumbed cake tin (about 23 cm in diameter).
• Rinse and halve the plums. Remove the stones and dip the cut surface in the sugar. Put the plums into the mixture with the peel side up.
• Pre-bake at 175° for about 10–15 minutes.

*Filling:*
• Whisk the cream. Mix in the egg and the sugar.
• Grate the lemon peel and chop the nuts roughly. Add this to the mixture.
• Pour the filling over the plums on the pre-baked cake. Bake for about a further 20 minutes until the cake has an attractive colour.

## Classic French apple tart

*(Tarte aux pommes)*

*A delicious apple tart that is simple to make. The generous amounts of butter make it melt in your mouth. Serve with lightly whipped cream.*

*Puff pastry:*
200 g butter
4 dl flour
2 tbsp cold water

*Filling:*
About 4 apples
75–100 g butter
Almost 1 dl sugar

To make the puff pastry, see the recipe for apple strudel on page 42. You can also use frozen puff pastry .

• Roll out the pastry and line a tart ring (about 23 cm in diameter).
• Prick the bottom with a fork and cover the edges with aluminium foil.
• Bake blind at 200° for 10 minutes.
• Peel, core and thinly slice the apples. Place the slices, overlapping, in a circular pattern.
• Melt the butter and brush generously over the apple slices. Sprinkle a little sugar over them. Repeat 2–3 times during baking.
• Bake the tart at 180–200° for about 25 minutes.

## Apple tart with nut filling

*For the real nut enthusiast. A crispy and juicy tart. Serve with whipped cream or full-cream ice.*

*Pastry:*
150 g butter
3 tbsp sugar
1 egg yolk
About 3 1/2 dl flour

*Filling:*
4-5 apples
100 g butter
75 g walnuts
75 g hazelnuts
50 g almonds
1 dl sugar
1 tbsp flour
3 tbsp milk

*Pastry:*
• Mix together all the ingredients for the pastry. Leave to chill for a while.
• Roll out the pastry and put it in a tart ring (about 23 cm in diameter). Prick the bottom with a fork and cover the edge with aluminium foil. Bake blind at 200° for about 5 minutes.

*Filling:*
• Peel, core and slice the apples. Put them in the tart base.
• Melt the butter and chop the nuts roughly.
• Mix all the ingredients and cover the apple slices with the mixture.
• Bake at 180° for about 30 minutes.

41

## Rosendal's apple strudel

*Real Apfelstrudel is a bit tricky to make, a whole science in fact. I make a simple one, which tastes just as good. We call it Rosendal's apple strudel.*

*Puff pastry:*
300 g butter
6 dl flour
4–6 tbsp cold water
(You can also use a packet of frozen puff pastry.)

*Filling:*
3 apples
2 dl brown sugar
1 1/2 dl crème fraiche
1/2 dl kesella
2 tsp cinnamon
2 dl raisins

*For glazing:*
1 egg

*Puff pastry:*
• Mix 1/4 of the butter with the flour and water. Work into a dough. Roll out into a rectangle.
• Slice the butter over one half of the pastry and fold over the other half. Press the edges together. Roll out again carefully, making sure that the butter does not come out. Then fold into three parts.
• Roll out again and repeat the procedure three times. This is easier if the pastry is left to chill between each rolling. Finally leave the pastry in the fridge.
• Roll out the pastry in half the brown sugar. Make sure the pastry is a bit shorter than the baking sheet.

*Filling:*
• Core and slice the apples really thin.
• Stir the other ingredients together and mix with the apples.
• Spread the filling along one side of the pastry. Roll up the strudel, turning in the ends, to make a long, thin roll. Brush with the egg.
• Bake at 225° for 15–20 minutes.

## Tarte Tatin

*A classic! This one is a little bit different with its whole apple halves. I make it in a cast-iron frying pan and turn it back into the pan before serving. You have to be careful not to burn yourself since the sugar liquid is really hot! Serve with whipped cream.*

*Puff pastry:*
200 g butter
About 4 dl flour
2–4 tbsp cold water
(You can also use a packet of frozen puff pastry.)

*Filling:*
100 g unsalted butter
2 1/2 dl sugar
Juice of 1/2 lemon
6 apples

*Puff pastry:*
• See apple strudel for making puff pastry.

*Filling:*
• Spread the butter evenly in a frying pan. Pour over sugar and lemon juice.
• Peel and core the apples and cut them in half. Put them with the round side downward in the frying pan.
• Roll out the pastry and wrap it round the rolling pin. Place the pastry over the apples in the frying pan. Pinch in the pastry inside the frying pan and trim off any pastry sticking out.
• Leave to chill for about 15 minutes.
• Turn on the oven at 200°.
• Heat up the hot plate. Put the frying pan on the hot plate, which should be really hot, for about 15 minutes until the butter and the sugar are bubbling and are golden in colour. Lift the edge occasionally with a small knife.
• Take the pan and place it in middle of the oven and bake for 10–15 minutes, until the cake is golden brown.
• Take the pan out of the oven. Note that the handle is very hot. Turn the cake out on to a plate and put it back in the frying pan.

## Signe's apple cake

*Cake:*
75 g butter
1 dl sugar
1 tbsp vanilla sugar
2 eggs
2 dl flour
1 tsp baking powder
4 large cooking apples, e.g. Signe Tillisch, James Grieve or similar

*Filling:*
2 eggs
3/4 dl sugar
2 tbsp vanilla sugar
1 1/2 dl crème fraiche

*Cake:*
• Peel, core, and cut the apples in segments. Put them in water with pressed lemon so they do not turn brown.
• Cream the butter, sugar and vanilla sugar until white and porous.
• Add the eggs, flour and baking powder.

Yellow and blue lemon cake. *Overleaf:* apple croissants, Tarte Tatin, classic French apple tart, 19th-century apple cake, apple strudel, apple burgers, apple and almond cake, apple tart with nut filling. Signe's apple cake and apple muffins.

• Pour the mixture into a greased and breadcrumbed cake tin with a high, detachable ring (about 23 cm in diameter). Smooth out the bottom with a spatula. Make sure some of the mixture goes up to the edge. Arrange the apple segments in circles in the cake tin.
• Bake at 175° for 20 minutes.

*Filling:*
• Whisk the eggs, sugar and vanilla sugar until white and fluffy. Fold in the crème fraiche.
• Spread the mixture over the cake and bake for another 30 minutes or until the cake has a good colour. Serve it with lightly whipped cream or Rosendal's home-made custard.

## 19th-Century apple tart

*There are recipes for many different kinds of apple cakes in older cookbooks. Apple cakes were often called apple pastries. This recipe is based on one for an "apple pastry" in Dr. Ch. Em. Hagdahl's cookery book from the 19th Century. This cake is great with whipped cream.*

*Pastry:*
4 dl flour
125 g butter
1 egg
1/2 dl sugar
2–4 tbsp cold water

*Filling:*
6 apples
5 tbsp cinnamon
1 1/2 dl sugar
2 tbsp vanilla sugar
125 g butter
1 1/2 dl almonds
2 bitter almonds
Peel of 1 lemon, grated
3 egg yolks
3 egg whites

*Pastry:*
• Chop the butter and the flour together. Add the sugar, egg and water. Work into pastry, using more water if necessary, and leave to chill for a few hours.
• Roll out the pastry and line a detachable tart ring (about 23 cm in diameter).
• Place in the fridge.

*Filling:*
• Peel and core the apples, and divide into segments.
• Melt 75 g butter in a frying pan. Add half the sugar, the apple slices and the cinnamon. Let the apple slices cook gently until soft. Stir occasionally.
• Cream the rest of the butter and sugar until white and porous. Grind the almonds and finely chop the bitter almonds. Whisk the egg whites until stiff.

• Carefully mix all the ingredients together, except the apples.
• Put the apples in the tart case and cover with the egg mixture.
• Bake the cake at 175° for about 45 minutes or until the surface is golden brown.

## Apple cake with almond

*If you have, like we do at Rosendal, an orchard with many beautifully coloured apples, you shouldn't need to peel them. Apples with their peel on give this cake its personality.*

5 eggs
2 dl sugar
1 dl icing sugar
150 g almond paste
2 tbsp cinnamon
About 4 dl flour
4 large apples
1 dl pearl sugar
75 g butter

• Whisk the egg, sugar and vanilla sugar until white and fluffy.
• Roughly grate the almond paste and stir together with the flour and cinnamon. Fold into the mixture. Pour the mixture into a greased and breadcrumbed tin (about 23 cm in diameter).
• Core and slice the apples thinly. Press the slices into the cake mixture. Sprinkle with pearl sugar. Slice the butter thinly with a cheese slicer and cover the cake with the slices.
• Bake at 180–200° for 45 minutes. Serve with our creamy custard.

## Sir James' apple cake

*This is a typical English cake. It is baked with whole wheat flour and demerara sugar, and has a delicious taste of nutmeg and cinnamon. It is quite chewy, so if you have a taste for the more fibrous this will become a favourite. Personally I like this cake best with a large dollop of whipped cream. The cake is named after the variety of the apple, James Grieve.*

*Cake:*
250 g butter
1 3/4 dl demerara sugar
3 eggs
4 dl whole wheat flour
1 tsp bicarbonate
1 tsp baking powder

Lemon tart. Sir James' apple cake. *Overleaf:* orange tart.

*Filling:*
150 g walnuts
150 g raisins
1 1/2 tsp ground nutmeg
1 1/2 tsp ground cinnamon
2 tbsp demerara sugar
3–4 cooking apples

*Cake:*
• Cream together the butter and the sugar. Add the eggs.
• In another bowl, stir together the flour, baking powder and bicarbonate.
• Add 2 1/2 dl of the flour mixture to the egg mixture. Save the rest for the filling.

*Filling:*
• Roughly chop the walnuts. Peel and core the apples and grate coarsely.
• Mix all the ingredients, except the demerara sugar, with the remaining flour mixture.
• Grease and breadcrumb a detachable baking ring with a high rim (about 23 cm in diameter).
• Spread out half the egg mixture into the ring. Spread on the filling and then pour over the rest of the egg mixture. Sprinkle with demerara sugar.
• Bake at 200° for about 60 minutes.

## Lemon tart

*This golden yellow, tangy tart is the perfect way to finish a dinner party. We serve it with whipped cream.*

*Pastry:*
3 1/2 dl flour
150 g butter
1 tbsp icing sugar
2 tbsp water

*Filling:*
Peel and juice of 3 lemons
3 eggs
1 1/2 dl sugar
1 dl double cream

*Pastry:*
• Mix the pastry ingredients together and leave to chill for at least an hour.
• Roll out the pastry and line a high-edged tart ring (about 23 cm in diameter). Prick the bottom with a fork and cover the edge with aluminium foil.
• Bake blind at 200° for about 10 minutes.

*Filling:*
• Grate the peel of the lemons and squeeze out the juice.
• Whisk the eggs and sugar until white and fluffy.
• Whisk the cream and fold into the egg mixture. Add the lemon peel and juice.
• Pour the mixture into the pre-baked tart case and bake at 180° for about 15 minutes.

## Yellow-and-blue lemon cake

*This juicy golden yellow cake is dotted with blue poppy seeds.*

175 g butter
3 dl sugar
2 eggs
Peel and juice of 1 lemon
2 tbsp candied orange peel
3/4 dl blue poppy seeds
2 dl flour
About 2 dl blue poppy seeds for sprinkling the greased cake tin

• Melt the butter and leave to cool somewhat.
• Stir in the sugar, eggs, lemon peel and juice, candied orange peel, poppy seeds and finally the flour.
• Pour the mixture into a greased cake tin (about 23 cm in diameter) which has been sprinkled with poppy seeds.
• Bake the cake at 180° for about 35 minutes.
• Powder the cake with icing sugar if you wish, and serve with whipped cream.

## Orange tart

*This delicious tart is red and yellow like the sun. Its sweet and sour taste goes well with whipped cream.*

*Pastry:*
150 g butter
1/2 dl sugar
1 egg yolk
4 dl flour
1 tsp baking powder

*Filling:*
3 egg yolks
1 dl sugar
Peel and juice of 1 orange
Segments of 4 oranges (2 blond and 2 blood oranges)

*Pastry:*
• Beat together the butter, sugar and egg yolks. Work in the flour mixed with baking powder.
• Press out the dough into a detachable pie ring with a high edge (about 23 cm in diameter). Press the pastry about 3 cm up the edge.
• Bake blind at 200° for about 10 minutes.

*Filling:*
• Whisk the egg yolks, sugar and orange juice in a saucepan and simmer on a low heat until the mixture has thickened. Do not allow to boil. Add the grated orange peel.
• Spread out the creamy mixture over the tart case. Place the skinless orange segments on top.
• Bake at 200° for 15–20 minutes.

## Banana and almond paste cake

2–3 bananas
5 eggs
3 dl sugar
150 g almond paste
3 1/2–4 dl flour
1 dl pearl sugar
75 g butter

• Peel and slice the bananas.
• Beat the egg and sugar until white and fluffy. Grate the almond paste and mix into the egg mixture, together with the flour.
• Pour the mixture into a greased and breadcrumbed cake ring (about 23 cm in diameter). Press down and spread the banana slices over the mixture. Sprinkle with pearl sugar and finally cover with slices of butter.
• Bake the cake at 175° for 30–40 minutes. Serve with lightly whipped cream.

## Apple bread
*(Makes 4 loaves)*

*A moist and tasty bread. It's very easy to bake and is attractively decorated, with a little red apple lighting up the middle.*

7 dl water
5 dl porridge oats (oat meal)
5 dl roughly grated apple
50 g fresh yeast
3 tsp salt
1 3/4–2 l flour, depending on how juicy the apples are

*For the glaze and decoration:*
4 small, red apples
1 egg

• Boil the water, pour it over the oats and stir. Roughly grate the apples and add.
• Dissolve the yeast in the lukewarm water.
• Add the salt and 1 3/4 l flour. Knead well until the dough is supple and shiny. Use more flour if necessary.
• Leave to rise under a cloth for about 60 minutes.
• Knead the dough again and divide into four pieces. Roll out each piece and tie into a simple knot. Put the loaves onto greased baking sheets and press a small red apple into the middle of each knot.

• Leave the bread to rise under a cloth for about 20–25 minutes. Set the oven to 225°. Brush the bread with the egg and place at the bottom of the oven. Immediately lower the oven to 200°.
• Bake for about 25 minutes. Knock the loaves on the bottom. They are ready if they sound hollow.

## Rhubarb compote with vanilla
*(Serves 4)*

800 g rhubarb
1 vanilla pod
1 dl sugar
1/2 dl water

• Rinse and peel the rhubarb, but only if the skin is really thick. Cut into pieces of about 4 cm.
• Split the vanilla pod and carefully remove the seeds with a small spoon. Keep the pod.
• Put the sugar, vanilla seeds, vanilla pod and the rhubarb alternately into a saucepan. Pour over the water.
• Simmer the compote on a very low heat under a lid for about 10 minutes. Flavour with a little extra vanilla sugar. Serve warm with whipped cream.

## Rhubarb and vanilla jam
*(About 1 1/2 litres)*

*Rhubarb is one of the first edible auguries of spring in the kitchen garden. To begin with the stalks are tender, pink and sour. This is the time to start serving the first rhubarb tarts of the season at the garden café. After a month or so, the rhubarb has grown thicker and I can begin my jam and marmalade making. This is a very easy recipe for a lovely, sticky jam. Serve with home-baked rusks or freshly toasted bread.*

1 kg rhubarb
1 kg sugar
2–3 vanilla pods (or 1 kg Rosendal's vanilla sugar)

• Clean and chop the rhubarb into smallish pieces. Split the vanilla pods and carefully remove the seeds with a small spoon.
• Put all the ingredients into a saucepan and simmer under a lid on a low heat. Stir occasionally so it does not stick to the pan. Remove the lid when the liquid from the rhubarb has boiled off, after about 20–30 minutes, depending on how juicy the rhubarb is. Boil for a further 40–60 minutes to a jam consistency. Stir occasionally.
• Scoop the jam into hot, well-cleaned jars and seal immediately.

## Plum jam with vanilla and walnuts
*(About 1 3/4 litres)*

1 2/3 kg plums
4 dl water
1 large vanilla pod
1 1/2 kg sugar
100 g roughly chopped walnuts

• Halve the plums and remove the stones. Put the plums in a pan with the water.
• Split the vanilla pod and remove the seeds. Put the vanilla pod and seeds into the pan and bring to the boil. Simmer on a low heat until the plums are soft.
• Stir in the sugar, a little at a time. Bring back to the boil and let the pulp simmer until it has thickened (about 20 minutes). Stir now and then, so that it does not stick to the bottom of the pan.
• Skim the jam carefully and stir in the chopped walnuts. Scoop up into hot, well-cleaned jars and seal straight away. Store in a cool place.

## Tangy orange marmalade
*(About 2 1/2 litres)*

1 kg thin-peeled oranges
2 lemons
1 l water
1 2/3 l sugar

• Rinse and brush the fruit well. Using a sharp knife, divide each orange and lemon into 8 segments. Then cut each segment into very thin slices. The thinner the slices, the finer the consistency of the marmalade.
• Put the orange and lemon segments into a jam-cooking pot. Pour over the water. Bring to the boil under a lid, but then remove the lid and allow to simmer for 30–35 minutes.
• Stir in the sugar, a little at a time. Make sure the sugar does not stick to the bottom of the pot.
• Boil the marmalade without a lid for about 25–40 minutes more. The length of time is dependent on the size of the pot and the amount of pectin in the oranges. Do the marmalade test when it begins to look ready. See page 214. Pour the marmalade into hot, well-cleaned jars and seal immediately.

Apricot jam with pistachio nuts and tangy orange marmalade. *Previous spread:* banana cake with almond paste.

# Apricot jam with pistachio nuts

*(8 jars of 200 ml each)*

*A very easy-to-make jam. We vary the nuts: sometimes we use pine kernels, walnuts, almonds or, as here, pistachios. The green of the pistachio nuts makes a pretty combination with the dark golden colour of the marmalade.*

1 kg dried apricots
Water
800–900 g sugar to each kg fruit pulp
Peel and orange of 2–3 large lemons
About 200 g shelled pistachios

- Put the apricots in water to swell overnight.
- Boil the apricots in their water until soft. This takes about 15–20 minutes.
- Pulp the fruit in a mixer. Weigh the pulp.
- Mix the pulp, sugar and lemon in a jam-making pot. Bring to the boil, stirring continuously so that it doesn't stick. Jam does stick very easily. Let it simmer slowly on a very low heat for a further 5–10 minutes.
- Stir in the pistachios or other nuts. Pour the jam into hot, well-cleaned jars and seal immediately.

# Candied orange peel

*Candied orange peel is excellent for all sorts of baking. I use it quite often in our cakes. It is definitely well worth your while making your own, since the bought kind has a drier consistency and does not give you such a moist cake. Keep the candied orange peel in preserving jars or freeze them in smaller portions.*

*Sugar-liquid for 1/2 kg orange peel:*
8 dl sugar
3 dl water
Strained juice of 1 squeezed lemon

- Peel the oranges finely and put the peel in water for about two days. Change the water occasionally.
- Put the peel into boiling water and boil until soft. Pour off the water and cut away the white of the peel with a small, sharp knife. Weigh the peel and chop quite finely.
- Bring to the boil the ingredients for the syrup of water. Put in the chopped peel and lower the heat. Simmer until the peel looks transparent. This takes about 45 minutes.
- Pour the peel and syrup of water into hot, well-cleaned jars or freeze them for later use.

Candied orange peel.

Sugar & vanilla

Vanilla. The exotic fruit of a tropical orchid. Its name, its unique shape and even the way it grows gives vanilla a very special appeal to me. The very name tastes delicious, vanilla. And just think of all the things you can use it for: vanilla hearts, vanilla custard, vanilla cream, vanilla pears. Yes, my mouth is watering already.

When I split a vanilla pod and carefully scrape out every tiny seed with my very special little vanilla spoon I think: "Oh, that there can be so much in this wonderful pod!"

We always use fresh, plump and generous vanilla pods at Rosendal. Nothing goes to waste. The empty pods are used as decoration for preserves or as a certificate of authenticity in the custard. And, of course, the pods are put in from the start when we boil pears or make custard.

Since I began making our own vanilla sugar I can't understand how anyone can manage without it. It is simple, and fun to make. There's an easy recipe in this chapter. The glass jar with your own vanilla sugar should have its given place beside the other jars of spiced sugar. The characteristic black seeds testify to its craftsmanship. The scooped out pods snuggle down in the white sugar. The taste of vanilla becomes full and distinct and the fragrance deliciously enticing.

Vanilla, *vanilla planifolia*, is a tropical orchid that comes originally from Mexico's hot and humid lowland. These days they are also grown in other places, such as the islands of the Indian Ocean. The leaves are fleshy and grow on long posts. The yellowish-white flowers come next, and are followed by that long, narrow, attractive fruit, the vanilla pod!

Unfortunately we cannot grow vanilla at Rosendal or anywhere in Sweden. But I still have a dream that one day I will harvest my very own vanilla pods.

*Opposite page:* syrup snips, sugar twist buns, sugar rusks, white vanilla sugar, sponge cake, vanilla pears & vanilla apples, vanilla custard and vanilla sugar made with demerara sugar.

## Sugar rusks

*(Makes about 160)*

*Good old-fashioned, little sugar rusks. I flavour them with cardamom and we sell them in our garden shop.*

1 dl sugar
7 dl flour
3 tsp baking powder
2–3 tsp newly crushed cardamom kernels
150 g butter
1 1/2 dl double cream

• Mix all the dry ingredients together. Save a little flour for the dough-making.
• Rub the butter into the flour. Add the cream and quickly work together.
• Form into small, round buns and put them on greased baking sheets.
• Bake at 200° for about 8 minutes.
• Divide the buns with a fork while they are still hot. Dry the rusks at 100° until they feel dry and are pale golden.

## Syrup snips

*(Makes about 40)*

200 g butter
1 3/4 dl sugar
2 tbsp golden syrup
2 tbsp vanilla sugar
5 dl flour
2 tsp baking powder

• Beat the butter, sugar and syrup until white and porous. Mix in the other ingredients.
• Turn out the dough onto a lightly floured surface and roll into lengths. Put them on a greased baking sheet.
• Bake the lengths at 160° for 12–15 minutes. Cut them into slices with a sharp knife before they have cooled completely.

## Sugar twist buns

*(Makes about 15)*

*These sugar twist buns are much appreciated at the garden café by young and old alike, maybe because the twist bun is the Swedish symbol for a confectionary baker. These twist buns are large and generous.*

200 g butter
6 tbsp double cream
5 1/2 dl flour

*For decoration:*
Pearl sugar

• Beat the butter soft. Add the cream and flour. Work into a supple dough.

• Roll out the pastry into narrow lengths and form into twists.

• Put the pearl sugar on a plate and dip the twists, top downward, into the sugar and press firmly so that the sugar fastens properly. Place the twists on a greased baking sheet.
• Bake at 200° for 12–15 minutes.

## Sponge cake

*Sponge cakes are probably the most commonly baked cake in Swedish homes. There are enormous numbers of different sponge cake recipes. In the old days you just used whatever you happened to have in the house. The resulting cake could be very simple or very refined. Here's a recipe for a moist sponge cake that can also serve as a cake bottom.*

4 eggs, the yolks and the whites separate
3 dl sugar
1 1/2 dl water
1 1/2 dl flour
1 1/2 dl potato flour
2 tsp vanilla sugar
2 tsp baking powder
Coconut to sprinkle the cake tin

• Beat together the egg yolks and the sugar. Add the water and whisk for a few minutes more.
• Mix together the flour, potato flour, vanilla sugar and baking powder and stir into the mixture.
• Whisk the egg whites and carefully fold them into the mixture. Mix well.
• Pour the mixture into a cake tin of about 2 litres, greased and sprinkled with coconut.
• Bake the cake at 175° for about 35 minutes.

## Rosendal's vanilla custard

*I always use real vanilla when I'm making vanilla custard at the garden café. Both our own vanilla sugar and sugar with vanilla pods give a good vanilla taste. Double cream gives a richer consistency. This custard is excellent with most apple cakes and pastries, but also with berry tarts and cakes.*

3 egg yolks
1 tbsp cornflour
3 dl double cream
3 tbsp Rosendal's vanilla sugar (or 2–3 tbsp sugar and a vanilla pod).

• Beat the egg yolks, cornflour and double cream in a stainless steel saucepan. Let simmer, but whisk continuously so that the custard doesn't stick.
• Remove the saucepan from the heat when the custard has the right thickness. Add vanilla sugar to taste.

## Vanilla cream

*(About 4 dl)*

*A thick and porous cream that I use as a filling in cakes and berry tarts. Sometimes I use vanilla cream instead of jam in our jam buns, thus making them vanilla buns instead. If there's any cream over, you can use it with fresh berries. It will keep in the fridge for a few days.*

3 egg yolks
3 dl double cream
1 1/2 tbsp potato flour
3 tbsp Rosendal's vanilla sugar (or 3 tbsp sugar and a vanilla pod)

• Beat the egg yolks and the cream in a stainless steel saucepan. Whisk in the potato flour and simmer on a low heat. Whisk continuously until the cream thickens.
• Add the vanilla sugar and whisk the cream until cold.

## Rosendal's vanilla sugar

*Your own vanilla sugar tastes great and it's easy and fun to make. I have a whole family of jars of different spiced sugars on one of the shelves in the café's kitchen. I use this tasty vanilla sugar for baking and for different sauces. The black vanilla seeds give it a pleasant and authentic appearance.*

5 fresh vanilla pods
1 kg sugar

• Make a slit in each pod. Carefully remove the seeds with a little spoon. Keep the pods.
• Stir the sugar and the vanilla seeds. Alternate the sugar and the pods in a pretty pattern in a glass jar. Put the lid on and allow to stand for at least two weeks.

## Dr. Hagdahl's vanilla apples

*This recipe is inspired by Dr. Ch. Em. Hagdahl's famous 19th-century book: The Art and Science of Cookery. Serve the apples hot with vanilla ice cream.*

1 kg apples
1 lemon
1 l water
9 dl sugar
2 vanilla pods

• Peel the apples, but leave the stalk. Put them into water with pressed lemon juice so that they do not go brown.
• Split the pods and carefully remove the vanilla seeds with a small spoon. Keep the pods.
• Boil the water, sugar and vanilla seeds. Stir until the sugar has dissolved.
• Add the apples and the vanilla pods and simmer on a low heat for 15–30 minutes depending on the variety of apple, their size and ripeness.

• Place the apples on a decorative plate and pour over some of the sugar-vanilla liquid. Serve the apples hot with full-cream ice.

## Rosendal's vanilla pears

*These pears are one of the highlights of the Christmas Fair, but they can be made at other times of the year when you feel inspired. Bottled pears are a dessert with a long history and they are very popular amongst Rosendal's visitors today.*

1 kg pears
1 l water
9 dl sugar
2 vanilla pods
1 lemon

• Peel the pears, leaving the stalk. Put them into water with pressed lemon juice so that they do not go brown.
• Split the pods and carefully remove the vanilla seeds with a small spoon. Keep the pods.
• Boil the water, sugar and vanilla. Stir until the sugar has dissolved.
• Add the pears and simmer for 15–30 minutes depending on the variety of pear, their size and ripeness. Take out the pears and serve with lightly whipped cream and some of the liquid. If you are going to serve the pears on another occasion, you can preserve them in glass jars. See page 213.

"Jordgubbar, indianer och annat."

På den tiden hade vi alla sorters bär, rabarber och fruktträd på ängen. I skogen fanns fullt av blåbär och lingon och på ängen kunde man också plocka blommor av alla de slag. Inte enbart gullviva, mandelblom, kattfot och blå viol, som det står i visan, utan även prästkrage, smörblomma, blåklocka, klöver och blåklint. Potatis, rädisor, grönsallad och morötter odlades i raka rader.

Mamma hade "gröna fingrar." Hon var nog mest rädd om sina rosenrabatter vid stugan, men allt som kunde gro på ängen var vid den här tiden viktigt för hushållet. Sallad, tomater, färska bär och frukter fick man njuta när säsongen bjöd och då gällde det också att sylta, safta och lägga in för vinterförrådet.

På sydsluttningen i dikesrenen växte smultron och på andra sidan vägen lyste vallmon i sädesfältet. Där hade jag sånär blivit halshuggen av slåttermaskinen en gång då jag låg på rygg och undersökte ett moget ax inne i den susande solbelysta härligheten. Bonden såg mig inte, men hästen tvärstannade.

Jordgubbar och hallon var frukter och de gula plommonen var spännande fram mot eftersommaren, fast björnbären var roligare att pilla på Hjöls jord. Där fanns större träd, som man kunde klättra i. Bonden bredde ut

2)

saltbössan några gånger, men jag tror, så här
i efterhand, inte att kråkskrämde inte på annat
än stjärnorna, för jag blev aldrig glödgad i
röven."

Våra täppor kunde naturligtvis inte bara
skördas, de måste gräras och rensas också.

Jag var lika osynlig när det gällde att
rensa ogräs som jag var synlig när det var
dags att skörda. Det krävdes också mycket
vatten, men brunnen var uttorkad, så om
mamma kallade med en spann i handen
var jag som uppslukad av naturen, oftast
gömd i ett närbeläget mulaget sandtag.

De gamla utgrävningarna hade med åren
förvandlats till ett veritabelt vilda västern
med glest bevuxna sandkullar och dalgångar
idealiska för bokfall. Där i det stora
krigets skugga utkämpades lekfulla strider
mellan "cowboys och indianer".

Men åter till täppan och ängen, där
jag väl när allt kommer omkring, till fågatorna
av mamma då och så fick använda tossorna
till att repa ogräs i jordgubbslandet.

Våra egna jordgubbar var naturligtvis
bäst, men de från Möja var sötare och de
finaste för öget och satt.

De mörkröda Möjagubbarna landades
från öppen fjärdskötbåt nere i vår vik
varifrån de bars i triumf upp till stugan.

Omgivande träd och buskar insveptes mer
i den himmelska söta doften från årets syltkok.

Ångor från byttorna på den ved eldade
spisen strömmade ut genom det öppna
köks fönstret och blandade sig med den
ljumma eftermiddagsbrisen. När doften
nådde "Vilda Västern" d.v.s. sandtaget
upphörde alla indiankrig, och strax, som
genom ett trollslag satt kombattanterna,
som plötsligt blivit väldigt hjälpsamma,
sida vid sida i matron och mosade mörja-
gubbar som stänktes med nyskummad grädde
från mjölkbyttan de tjänstvilligt och i
hast hade tänkat hem från bondgården.

Så kunde en sommarkväll sluta, på
den tiden vi hade tro och blommor och
frukt-tänd på ögen.

Vilcken
TÅRTA!

Sven-Bertil Taube

Din Tigerkaka smakar
tio gånger bättre
än mammas !
(men säg inget till
mamma !)

Chocolate & Cacao

Chocolate is something to Love. Most people have a very special relationship with chocolate. Some people eat it, possibly far too much, when they in a state of depression, others eat it, maybe not quite so much, when they are in a state of euphoria. But there are, in fact, people who know how to enjoy it in just the right amounts, this fantastic offspring of the cocoa bean.

As for myself, I have all sorts of reasons for falling for chocolate. I am, of course, in the company of this ambrosia, *Theobroma cacao*, every day. It can be in the form of chocolate cake batter, which gives me a reason to lick the bowl, or maybe the reason is in the form of our French chocolate cake which, together with a large dollop of cream, is an almost phenomenal taste sensa-tion. Whatever else I may have eaten previously, I can almost never resist taking at least one little piece of our almost dementedly delicious white chocolate mousse cake.

You can't hide your lust for chocolate. The signs are just too disdainfully obvious. If it is hot, the chocolate melts and gets messy. If it is cold, the chocolate goes hard and crumbles. And whatever the weather, the contours round the lips of both our customers and ourselves are proof of what we have been consuming. That chocolate coloured contour, on both large and small, revealing the lusts that we just can't resist. So maybe we should count ourselves fortunate that we can't grow cocoa trees in this part of the world!

*Overleaf:* A. Chocolate and orange squares. B. Dream cake. C. French sticky chocolate cake, glazed chocolate squares and fine French sticky chocolate cake. D. Chocolate-chip cookies. E. Chocolate cake with chocolate sauce. F. Chocolate and orange cake. G. Chocolate snips. H. White chocolate mousse gâteau.

## Chocolate snips

*(Makes about 45)*
*A classic cake with a full chocolate flavour.*

200 g butter
2 1/2 dl sugar
5 dl flour
5 tbsp cocoa
1 tsp baking powder
1 tbsp vanilla sugar
1 egg

*For decoration or glaze:*
Egg and pearl sugar

• Cream the butter and sugar together. Mix in the other ingredients.
• Turn out on to a floured surface and roll into lengths. Put these on a greased baking sheet. If you wish you can brush with egg and sprinkle with pearl sugar.
• Bake at 180° for about 12 minutes.
• Cut the lengths into "snips" before they have cooled completely. Store in a dry place.

## Chocolate-chip cookies

*(Makes about 25–40 depending on size)*

*An American classic. There's no end of recipes for these much loved biscuits. I make them as big as tea-plates for our garden café. But when I bake them for the garden shop I make them smaller and easier to handle.*

3 dl flour
1 tsp salt
1 tsp bicarbonate
190 g butter
4 1/2 dl brown sugar
3/4 dl sugar
1 tsp vanilla sugar
2 eggs
6 1/2 dl porridge oats (oat meal)
350 g dark Belgian cooking chocolate, roughly chopped

• Mix the flour, bicarbonate and salt in a bowl.
• Cream together the brown sugar, sugar, vanilla sugar and butter in another bowl.
• Lightly whisk the eggs. Add to the sugar and butter mixture, with the oats. Mix well. Add the flour mixture and mix well by hand. Finally add the chopped chocolate. Drop the mixture onto greased baking sheets.
• Bake at 150–180° for 8–12 minutes, according to size.

## Chocolate and orange squares

*This is my own flat and sticky version of the classic Brownie. Powder with icing sugar to decorate before serving.*

150 g butter
2 eggs
3 dl sugar
Grated peel and juice of 1 orange
3/4 dl milk
3/4 dl double cream
4 1/2 dl flour
2 tsp vanilla sugar
4–5 tbsp cocoa
1 1/2 tsp baking powder
50–75 g dark Belgian cooking chocolate

• Melt the butter and leave to cool.
• Whisk the egg and sugar until white and fluffy.
• Grate and squeeze the orange. Mix the peel and the juice together with the milk-and-cream and add to the egg mixture.
• Stir together the flour, vanilla sugar, cocoa and baking powder. Add to the mixture alternately with the melted butter.
• Chop the chocolate quite finely and mix in.
• Pour the mixture into a greased and breadcrumbed roasting tin.
• Bake the cake at 150° for 20–25 minutes. Cut into squares and serve if you wish with a little blob of whipped cream.

## Glazed chocolate squares

*This cake is also called Martha cake, and it is a real childhood memory for most Swedes. Everyone seems to have eaten it at some time and would like to try it again. This is one of the café's most requested cakes. This recipe comes from my childhood and many of the measurements are in cups (1 cup=1 1/2 dl).*

*Cake:*
150 g butter
2 eggs
2 cups sugar
1 cup milk
3 cups flour
2 tsp baking powder
2 tsp vanilla sugar
1 1/2 tbsp cocoa

*Glaze:*
2 1/2 cups icing sugar
4 tbsp butter
5 tbsp cold coffee
1 1/2 tbsp cocoa
2 tsp vanilla sugar
Coconut to sprinkle

*Cake:*
• Melt the butter.
• Whisk the egg and sugar until white and fluffy.
• Stir together the flour, baking powder, vanilla sugar and cocoa. Add to the egg-and-sugar mixture alternately with the butter and the milk.
• Pour into a greased and breadcrumbed roasting tin.
• Bake at 200° for about 20 minutes.

*Glaze:*
• Melt the butter. Add the other ingredients and stir well until smooth. Spread the glaze over the cake and sprinkle with coconut. Cut into squares.

## Dream cake

*This cake tastes like a dream, just as the name suggests. Use generous amounts of buttercream.*

*Cake:*
3 eggs
1 1/2 dl sugar
Almost 1 dl potato flour
2 tbsp cocoa
1 tsp baking powder

*Buttercream:*
150 g butter
3 1/2 dl icing sugar
2 egg yolks
1 tbsp vanilla sugar

*Cake:*
• Whisk the egg and sugar until white and fluffy.
• Add the potato flour, cocoa and baking powder. Mix well.
• Spread the mixture over greaseproof paper in a roasting tin.
• Bake at 200° for 5 minutes.

*Buttercream:*
• Cream the butter. Add the egg yolks, icing sugar and vanilla sugar. Mix vigorously into a fluffy cream for spreading on the cake when cooled.
• Roll up the cake from the long side by "pulling the paper". Cut into large, generous slices.

## Tiger cake

*Striped like a tiger, moist, filling and big enough to feed the whole family... The tiger cake is one of our most requested cakes.*

200 g butter
2 dl sugar
2–3 tbsp vanilla sugar
3 eggs
80–100 g candied orange peel
Juice of 1 orange
5–6 dl flour
1 1/2 tsp baking powder
1 1/2 dl double cream
1 dl cocoa

• Cream together the butter and sugar until white and porous. Add the eggs one at a time. Then add the candied orange peel and the orange juice.
• Stir the baking powder into the flour. Add to the mixture, alternately with the cream.
• Spoon out about half the mixture into a large, round, greased and breadcrumbed baking tin with a hole in the middle. The tin should hold at least 2 litres.
• Stir the cocoa into the remaining mixture. Spread the dark mixture over the light. Rake round the mixture with a fork to make the stripes.
• Bake at 175° for about 40 minutes. Test with a skewer to see if the cake is ready. Turn off the oven but leave the cake in it for a few minutes.

## Chocolate and orange cake

*Chocolate and orange is a famous combination. Our orange-flavoured chocolate cake is wonderfully dark and very moist. Serve with a blob of cream.*

200 g butter
2 1/2 dl sugar
6 tbsp cocoa
Juice and peel of a smallish orange
3 eggs
About 4 1/2 dl flour
1 tsp baking powder
1 dl double cream
100 g dark Belgian cooking chocolate, roughly chopped

• Cream together the butter and sugar. Stir in the cocoa, the grated orange peel and the orange juice. Add the eggs one at a time.
• Mix the flour and baking powder. Fold this into the egg mixture, alternately with the cream. Finally add the lightly floured chocolate.
• Pour the mixture into a greased and breadcrumbed ring-shaped baking tin, that should hold at least 1 1/2 litres.
• Bake the cake at 175° for about 45 minutes.

# French sticky chocolate cake

*The easiest, the tastiest and the stickiest... The small blue poppy seeds give this cake a very distinctive appearance. Of course you can bake the cake without the poppy seeds if you want.*

100 g butter
3 dl sugar
2 eggs
2 tsp vanilla sugar
5 tbsp cocoa
3/4 dl blue poppy seeds
1 1/2 dl flour
A pinch of salt
Blue poppy seeds for the cake tin

- Mix all the ingredients into the melted butter.
- Pour the mixture into a greased and poppy sprinkled baking tin (about 23 cm in diameter). Spread the mixture right out to the edges. Use a wide bladed knife or the cake can be uneven.
- Bake at 175° for about 30 minutes. Powder with icing sugar before serving. Serve with whipped cream.

# Fine French sticky chocolate cake

*A more exclusive sticky cake, with a rich and full chocolate flavour.*

225 g dark Belgian cooking chocolate
225 g butter
4 eggs
2 dl sugar
2 1/2 dl flour
1 tsp baking powder
About 2 dl chopped walnuts for sprinkling the greased cake tin

- Melt the cooking chocolate and the butter on a low heat in a thick-bottomed saucepan. Leave to cool somewhat.
- Whisk the egg and sugar until white and fluffy.
- Mix the flour and the baking powder. Stir the chocolate-and-butter mixture into the egg-and-sugar mixture. Fold in the flour and stir – not too vigorously – into a smooth mixture.
- Pour the mixture into a greased cake tin, sprinkled with chopped walnuts. The tin should have a detachable bottom and be about 23 cm in diameter.
- Bake at 200° for 25 minutes. The cake should be a little sticky in the middle even when fully baked. Serve with whipped cream.

# Toffee gâteau

*Cake:*
30 g almonds
50 g walnuts
50 g hazelnuts
1 3/4 dl sugar
2 eggs
1 1/3 dl flour
1 tsp baking powder
1 tsp icing sugar
1 dl double cream

*Toffee cream:*
1 1/2 dl sugar
2 tbsp cocoa
75 g butter
1 dl double cream

*Cake:*
- Grind the nuts finely.
- Whisk the egg and sugar until white and fluffy. Mix in the flour, baking powder, vanilla sugar, nuts and finally the cream. Pour the mixture into a greased and breadcrumbed cake tin (about 23 cm in diameter).
- Bake the cake at 175° for about 30 minutes.

*Toffee cream:*
- Melt the butter and mix in the other ingredients. Boil until a thick cream. Stir occasionally.
- Cut the cake in half. Spread the somewhat cooled toffee cream between the halves and on top. Serve with whipped cream.

# Chocolate cake with chocolate sauce

*This cake has a generous chocolate flavour and is glazed with real chocolate sauce. Serve the cake with whipped cream.*

*Cake:*
100g butter
1 1/2 dl milk
2 eggs
3 dl sugar
3 dl flour
2 tsp baking powder
2 1/2 tbsp cocoa
1 tbsp vanilla sugar

*Chocolate sauce:*
50 g butter
1 dl milk
1 1/2 tsp flour
2 tbsp sugar
1 tbsp cocoa
Coconut for sprinkling

*Cake:*
• Melt the butter and mix with the milk. Heat to lukewarm.
• Whisk the egg and sugar until white and fluffy.
• Stir together the flour, baking powder, cocoa and vanilla sugar and add to the egg mixture alternately with the milk mixture. Pour the batter into a greased and breadcrumbed cake tin (about 23 cm in diameter).
• Bake at 175° for about 30 minutes.

*Chocolate sauce:*
• Melt the butter and pour in the milk.
• Mix the flour and sugar with the cocoa. Add the mixture to the saucepan whilst stirring and boil into a fairly thick sauce. Stir continuously so that the sauce doesn't stick.
• Spread the sauce over the cake when it has cooled somewhat, and sprinkle with coconut.

# White chocolate mousse gâteau

*Cake:*
400 g almond paste
4 eggs
4 tbsp cocoa
Grated peel of 1 orange

*Filling:*
300 g white Belgian chocolate
6 dl double cream
4 egg yolks

*For decoration:*
Raspberry sauce is excellent with this cake. See page 27.

*Cake:*
• Grate the almond paste and the orange peel. Mix with the eggs and the cocoa.
• Spread the mixture into a greased detachable cake ring (about 23 cm in diameter).
• Bake at 175° for about 20 minutes.

*Filling:*
• Melt the chocolate in a bain-marie. Allow to cool somewhat but stir continuously so it doesn't go lumpy.
• Whip the cream and mix it into the somewhat cooled chocolate. Mix in the egg yolks, one at a time.
• Pour the mixture into the cake ring and place in the freezer for a couple of hours.
• Take out the cake about 40 minutes before serving. Make the raspberry sauce and lay like a lake under each slice, or under the whole gâteau.

French sticky chocolate cake, toffee gâteau and chocolate glazed French sticky chocolate cake.

Butter, Milk,
Cream & Eggs

It just has to be butter! Butter is natural and has a fine consistency and flavour. My grandfather, who was a baker, would never have dreamt of making buttercream with anything but butter. That wonderful butter taste is particularly important in biscuits and cookies.

Buttercups, butterballs, butter buns and butter wreaths, they all have agreeable names that fill you with pleasure. Sometimes, during a busy spring Sunday, we "forget" the cream that is being whipped. But what does that matter, for who would want to miss the excited cries from the girls and boys at the café: "We've made butter! We've made butter!" You just have to add a little salt and the butter is ready to put on the table.

Milk should be the "red" kind, as my generation in Sweden calls it, that is to say the milk with the highest percentage of fat. Whether you use it for coffee, in the cake mixture or with the cakes themselves. What can taste better with a newly baked bun than a glass of cold milk?

The cream is always double cream. This gives you a moist cake, a full-flavoured soup and a rich, smooth sauce. We sometimes have some whipped cream left over at the end of the day. But if we add some Dijon mustard or freshly grated horseradish to it, this will give us an appetising sauce for the smoked ham the following day.

Eggs are beautiful, I think. There are few foodstuffs that can be used for so much. Whole eggs, or egg whites and yolks on their own can be used in an endless variety of baking. Eggs sometimes present certain problems, since the eggs we use at Rosendal come from happy hens that lay eggs in all sorts of sizes. There can be one or three yolks inside an egg, so when I'm baking something with eighty eggs I have to keep track of the numbers since I can't count the yolks afterwards. This is why I almost always measure the eggs in a litre measuring jug nowadays. One piece of wisdom I can share with you is this, that four egg whites are a decilitre and one normal yolk is a tablespoon.

*Overleaf:* meringue snips, aunt Hikkla's cottage cheese cake, butter-filled whole wheat buns and filled petits-choux.

## Meringue snips

*(Makes about 25)*

*Small, crispy, delicate old-fashioned "snip" cakes. They are practical to make when you have a lot of egg whites left over. They taste great with a glass of fruit juice.*

*Cake:*
100 g butter
1/2 dl sugar
2 1/2 dl flour

*Meringue:*
2 egg whites
1 dl sugar
1 dl chopped almond

• Cream together the butter and sugar until white and porous. Add the flour. Work into a dough. Roll out the dough into two lengths and place on a greased baking sheet.
• Bake at 200° for about 15 minutes.
• Lower the oven to 150°.
• Whisk the egg whites vigorously into a foam. Add the sugar and whisk for another minute or so. Chop the almonds.
• Spread the meringue on the lengths and sprinkle with the almonds.
• Bake at 150° for 5–10 minutes until the meringue is pale golden. Cut the lengths into slanting "snips".

## Filled petits-choux

*(Makes about 12–15)*

*This is a greatly appreciated dessert at our buffets. Our petits-choux are filled with in-season berries, banana and whipped cream. They can also be baked in the shape of a wreath by placing them in a circle on the baking sheet.*

*Cake:*
2 dl water
60 g butter
2 dl flour
3 eggs

*Filling:*
3 dl double cream
1/2 l raspberries and blueberries mixed
1 banana sliced thin
Grated chocolate

• Boil the water and the butter. Stir in the flour. Boil up the mixture whilst stirring vigorously and allow to boil until it comes away from the edge of the saucepan. Stir briskly the whole time.
• Remove from the heat and stir until the mixture has cooled. Add the eggs one at a time, whisking briskly between each egg.
• Drop the mixture in balls onto a greased baking sheet.

• Bake at 200° for about 20–25 minutes. Do not open the oven door until they are ready. Remove the petits-choux and allow to cool.
• Halve the petits-choux and fill them with them with the cream, berries, and banana. Grate a little chocolate over and put on the "lid".

## Aunt Hilkka's cottage cheese cake

*My uncle is married to Hilkka who comes from Finland, where it is quite common to use fresh cheese in baking. Aunt Hilkka's cottage cheese cake is best eaten newly baked.*

*Cake:*
75 g butter
1 1/2 dl milk
25 g fresh yeast
1/2 dl sugar
4 1/2 dl flour

*Filling:*
1 egg
1/2 dl sugar
250 g cottage cheese
1 tbsp flour
1/2 dl raisins
Grated peel of 1 lemon

*For glazing:*
1 egg

• Melt the butter. Pour into the milk and heat to luke-warm. Dissolve the yeast in the liquid and add the sugar and flour. Knead into a dough and leave to rise under a cloth for about 30 minutes.
• Whisk the egg and sugar until white and fluffy. Add the cottage cheese, flour, raisins and grated lemon peel.
• Roll out about 3/4 of the dough. Line the bottom and the edges of a greased flan ring (about 23 cm in diameter). Pour in the filling. Roll out the rest of the dough and cut into lengths to make a lattice over the filling. Leave to rise for 30 minutes. Brush with the whisked egg.
• Bake at 200° for about 25 minutes.

## Butter filled whole wheat buns

*(Makes about 20–25)*

*These buns are also called Rosendal's buns. They look extraordinarily wholesome. But appearances are deceptive. They contain lots of butter and sugar. They are somewhat hard in consistency. An unusual fun bun.*

*Buns:*
9 dl whole wheat flour
1 dl flour
30 g fresh yeast
2 dl milk
1 tsp salt

50 g butter
2 eggs, lightly whisked

*Filling:*
150 g soft, spreadable butter
150 g raisins
2 dl demerara sugar

*For glazing and decoration:*
Melted butter
Blue poppy seeds
Ground cinnamon

• Heat the milk to lukewarm. Dissolve the yeast and add about 2 dl whole wheat flour. Leave to stand in a warm place, free from draughts, until the mixture begins to bubble.
• Mix the rest of the flour with the salt. Rub in the butter and add the lightly beaten eggs with the yeast mixture. Knead well.
• Divide the dough into two pieces. Roll out each piece into a rectangle.
• Spread the butter over each rectangle, covering as much as possible. Sprinkle with raisins and sugar.
• Roll up each rectangle like a swiss roll. Cut the rolls into about 20–25 pieces. Put the buns with the cut side up in a greased roasting pan.
• Leave to rise until they are higher than the edge, about 20–30 minutes.
• Brush the buns with melted butter and sprinkle with blue poppy seeds and ground cinnamon.
• Bake at 200° for about 20–25 minutes.

# Egg bread
*(Two small or one large loaf)*

*I make this bread for the shop at Easter. I put an egg right in the middle, both for fun and for decoration. We sometimes have small, newly laid eggs to put there. The bread is brushed with beaten egg and powdered with turmeric to give it a yellow, Easter look.*

50 g fresh yeast
6 dl water
2 tsp sugar
2 tsp salt
3 dl whole wheat flour
About 1 l flour

*For glaze and decoration:*
1 egg + 1–2 eggs
Turmeric

• Dissolve the yeast in the lukewarm water.
• Add the sugar, salt, whole wheat flour and the other flour, a little at a time. Knead the dough well and leave to rise under a cloth for about 45 minutes.
• Knead the dough again. Form into one or two lengths and make a simple knot. Place the bread on a greased baking sheet. Put an unboiled egg in the middle and leave to rise for 20 minutes.
• Brush the bread with beaten egg and powder with a little turmeric.
• Put the bread into a 250° oven, but reduce immediately to 225° and bake for about 15–25 minutes depending on the size of the loaf. Tap the bread underneath, if it sounds hollow then the bread is ready.

Lennartkaka

En lagom tung och väl avvägd kaka med
konsistens och viss doft av lerjord om våren.
I den långa eftersmaken ryms en bitter fruktig-
het som ger associationer till jul och ört-
kryddat vin.

Denna kaka smakar bäst efter en måltid med vilda ingredienser som exempelvis
helstekt hare med kantareller och rörörda
lingon. Äts med fördel till en kopp starkt
kaffe med het mjölk eller möjligen en
dubbel expresso. Med sitt ursprung i den
svenska myllan fullföljer denna kaka en
tradition i linje med gamla svenska
gästgivargårdar.

# Images of bread

As I am standing in the bread section of the department store, trying to work out which of the half-invisible objects behind the plastic wrappings can be a tasty and wholesome loaf, a young man dressed in the store's colourful shirt comes up beside me. He begins to pick amongst the bread, no, not pick: he *claws* about amongst the loaves, pulling them out one at a time, inspects them for a moment, and then throws them back on the shelf. Suddenly a loaf lands on the floor.

I presume that he's going to pick it up. But no! The procedure continues: pull out the package, inspect it, throw it back on the shelf – or let it fall on the stone floor with a thud. A little thud, and a slight rustle of plastic.

"Why are you doing that?" I ask.

"Expired," says he.

"But why are you throwing it on the floor?"

"A trolley's coming." Says he.

But the trolley dawdles, and a lot of loaves begin to collect on the floor. And it's narrow between the shelves and there's a lot of people in the store. So there's an ever greater risk that someone is going to tread in... *that*. For what is lying there now? A pile of dead bread.

For it is no longer good, living – I was just about to say: Holy bread? I can't stand to be there any longer. I don't care what's inside all those packages any longer. All those products with their fanciful names! With their perfect shapes, perfect mixtures! Baked in perfect ovens! Perfect products untouched by human hand!

My mother had two ovens for baking: one in the wood-fired stove in the kitchen, and one in the black gas oven that stood on top of the stove. She needed both. We were a large family. She did the weekly baking every Friday. Lovely, large round loaves that were dished out to us according to our ages and needs.

The only measure she used was an old teacup. And she mixed the dough and added flour from different bags with such prodigious ease that it never looked like an *art*. And she kneaded the dough and cut it into suitable pieces to roll into buns and then flatten out. They became the large, promising loaves that rose on baking sheets before they were rattled into the ovens.

A wood-fired oven. And a gas oven.

She never opened the oven doors until the bread was ready. Then out came the loaves. Golden brown.

Not completely perfectly shaped, not absolutely circular. Not exactly the same colour, but varied according to how close to the heat they had stood.

But bread, living bread!

And always enough!

Not a loaf too few or too many!

And as my elder siblings left home one after the other, those same experienced hands kept kneading the dough, although the number of loaves grew fewer. Finally she only needed to use the gas oven, which was easier to look after. And it was still bread.

Good, living bread!

But sometimes, oh, sometimes! When it was time for baking fancy biscuits and the sugar bag came out, and the cocoa packet, and the light butter, and the rolling-pin, and that flowery teacup with no handle (which was the measure of everything on *such* ceremonious occasions!) and the knife came out, the one which cut the sweet dough into straight lines like a map of Africa, *then* everything was almost as perfect as in a proper Bakery – except along the edges which had to be straightened with fingers – this was when we children could help at last!

Thus we always unmask ourselves.

To reveal how imperfect, inelegant we are, putting our fingerprints on those small biscuits, those love cookies, to make them come alive, touched by a human hand!

*Kent Andersson.*

Mother's long-bun.

Flour & Grain

The transformation that flour has to go through in order to be bread, a cake or a flan, is usually called baking. To be, as I am, a baker and to bake at Rosendal's café is to be a craftsman, with everything that involves. You have to use all your senses, have a certain amount of artistic creativity, sensitivity, and a great amount of imagination and spontaneity. We soon smell the well-known scent of newly baked bread, buns and flans.

The flour is fundamental to the character of the bread and these days there are many different kinds of kinds of flour, with different grades of fineness. Flour and grain have a very low water content and therefore keep very well. They are best stored in a dry and airy place.

The most usual kinds of flour come from wheat, rye, barley and oats. You can also get ready-made mixtures of different kind of grain. When I bake bread I often mix different kinds of flour in order to get a richer bread. Certain kinds of flour, such as barley, should be mixed with wheat or rye flour if they are to be used in fermenting doughs. This flour is often used in crispbread and "thinbread".

There is a whole range of flour or grain sorts that are, quite simply, more or less just starch. For example buckwheat, potato flour or cornflour. These can be good for gluten allergy sufferers to use.

It is always better to mix in a little of the flour first and work in the rest afterwards. This is particularly important since there are so many different kinds of flour available and they all behave differently. It is always easy to add a little more flour if necessary.

This text perhaps is a bit too matter-of-fact concerning, as it does, the most sensual of things in a baker's proximity, flour. That wonderful flour, that is so often the secret weapon in our baking personality.

Karin's Brogård crispbread.

# Oat crispies

*(Makes about 15)*

*Tasty, toffeeish crispies. Nice to serve with ice cream.*

100 g butter
2 dl porridge oats (oat meal)
1 1/2 dl sugar
Scant 1/2 dl golden syrup
2 tbsp double cream
1 dl flour
1 tsp baking powder
1 egg

*For decoration:*
Melted cooking chocolate

• Melt the butter and pour it over the oats. Leave for a few minutes.
• Stir in the sugar, syrup, cream, flour mixed with baking powder and finally the eggs.
• Bake at 175° for about 8–10 minutes.
• Melt the chocolate in a bain-marie. Dip a fork in the chocolate and "paint" the crispies.

# Melting moments

*(Makes about 25)*

*I found this recipe in an English magazine. These biscuits are very common in England. It was the beautiful name alone that enticed me to try to bake some. But when they were introduced at the café they became very popular.*

300 g butter
3 dl demerara sugar
1 egg, lightly beaten
1 vanilla pod
3 1/4 dl whole wheat flour
Almost 2 tsp baking powder
1 1/2 dl porridge oats (oat meal)
Extra oats to roll the biscuits in

• Cream together the sugar and butter until porous. Stir in the lightly beaten egg.
• Split open the vanilla pod and carefully scrape out the seeds. Mix them into the egg mixture with the flour, oat flakes and baking powder.
• Work the dough into walnut-sized balls and roll them in the porridge oats. Put the balls, widely spaced, onto a greased baking sheet and flatten them somewhat.
• Bake at 180° for about 15–20 minutes.

# Oat cakes

*(Makes about 12–15)*

*Dainty oat cakes with a lovely buttery taste. They look like little buns.*

150 g butter
3 dl porridge oats (oat meal)
3/4 dl sugar
3/4 dl raisins
1 1/2 dl flour
1 tsp bicarbonate

• Melt the butter. Pour it over the oats. Stir together and leave for a few minutes.
• Mix in the sugar, raisins and finally the flour mixed with the bicarbonate. Drop the cakes onto a greased baking sheet.
• Bake at 200° for 15–20 minutes.

# Carlsbad buns

*(Makes about 10–15)*

*Golden brown, smooth buns with a taste of cardamom. Eat them freshly baked with a glass of cold milk.*

100 g butter
2 dl milk
30 g fresh yeast
1/2 tsk salt
1 dl sugar
4 egg yolks
About 7 dl flour
1–2 tsp freshly crushed cardamom

• Melt the butter and add the milk.
• Dissolve the yeast in the lukewarm liquid.
• Add sugar, salt, egg yolks, cardamom and flour. Knead the dough well. Try to have as "loose" a dough as possible. Though it should come away from the edge of the bowl.
• Cover the dough with a little flour. Leave to rise under a cloth for about 45 minutes.
• Knead the dough thoroughly again. Add more flour if necessary. Shape into round, smooth buns, that is, the most difficult of bun types. Use the palm of your hand. Place the buns on greased baking sheets. Brush with egg and leave to rise under a cloth for 15–20 minutes.
• Bake the buns at 225–250° for 8–10 minutes.

# Mother's long-buns

*My mother used to make these long-shaped buns at least once a week when I was a child. When our guests had been asking for buns for a couple of years, I started to bake these long buns. They are cut into generous oblique pieces when they are served at the café. Sometimes we sell the whole lengths, warm and freshly baked, at the garden shop.*

150 g butter
5 dl milk
50 g fresh yeast
1/2 tsp salt
1 1/2 dl sugar
1 egg
About 1 1/3 l flour

*Filling:*
150 g butter
1 dl sugar
1/2 dl ground cinnamon

*For glazing or decorating:*
Egg
Pearl sugar

• Melt the butter, add the milk and heat to lukewarm.
• Dissolve the yeast in the liquid. Add sugar, salt, eggs and most of the flour. Knead thoroughly until the dough leaves the edge of the bowl.
• Sprinkle with flour and leave under a cloth to rise for 40–45 minutes.
• Turn out the dough and knead well. Divide it into 3–4 pieces. Roll out each piece into a rectangle.
• Vigorously mix all the ingredients for the filling. Spread over the rectangles using a butter knife.
• Roll up the dough from the long side. Put the lengths on a greased baking sheet with the join downwards. Cut flaps in the dough with a sharp knife. Fold over the flaps alternately to the left and to the right. Leave to rise under a cloth for about 25 minutes.
• Brush with the whisked egg and sprinkle with pearl sugar.
• Bake at 225° for about 15–20 minutes in the lower part of the oven.

# Karin's Brogård crispbread

*Home-baked crispbread is amongst the most delicious things I know. This is a crunchy bread made with rye flour and sifted rye flour, spiced with freshly crushed aniseed and fennel.*

50 g butter
2 dl water
50 g fresh yeast
1 tsp salt
2 tbsp fennel
1 tbsp aniseed
3 dl coarse rye flour
2 dl sifted rye flour

*For kneading:*
Flour

• Melt the butter. Pour in the water and heat to lukewarm.
• Dissolve the yeast in the liquid. Crush the spices with the salt in a mortar. Add them to the liquid with the rye flour. Knead the dough until supple and leave to rise under a cloth for about one hour.
• Turn out the dough onto a floured surface. Divide it into two parts. Roll out each part into a length and divide each length into 15–16 pieces. Shape each piece into a ball and then roll out thinly, first with an ordinary rolling-pin and then with a peg rolling-pin. Use quite a lot of flour when rolling.
• Bake the bread on greased baking sheets at 275° in the middle of the oven for about 5 minutes. If the bread is not thoroughly dry after baking, you can dry it further at 75°.

*Opposite page:* A. Melting moments and oak cakes. B. Oat crispies. C. Carlsbad buns.

Nuts

Just think what curious things nuts are: they all lie protected inside their shells, whatever their colour, shape or taste. The first association I, and maybe most people, have when the subject of nuts comes up, is of Christmas nuts. They lie there as a beautiful decoration, usually untouched, right up until Christmas Day. Then the walnuts seem to go first, and after them the more difficult to crack Brazil nuts and almonds, and if it wasn't for playing Philippines the hazelnuts would remain in their shells right until the end of January.

In recent years I have had only walnuts in my nut bowl, which has meant that I have used up the ones that were left over. I crack them and mix them into a cake or a jam with excellent results.

The characteristic flavour of nuts makes them a very rewarding ingredient in many of my favourite recipes. A chocolate cake gets a new taste with walnuts in it, an apple cake is made more interesting with bitter almonds, and sweet almonds are well suited to berry tarts. There are endless variations, so just let your fancy and imagination run amok.

But there is of course, this thing with allergies. Sometimes a guest wants to know which cakes contain nuts.

Usually it's great fun to go out to the cake table in the glasshouse and talk about the cakes. About which nuts they contain. If there is butter or cream in them. If they contain red currants or blackcurrants and not lingonberries, or vice versa. That this one is in fact a carrot cake, or that one which looks like a gingerbread cake is in fact a courgette cake. The questions are many and the interest great. Everyone wants an answer, so that they can choose which cake to eat. But a guest wanting to know which cakes contain nuts can block the queue and create confusion on a sunny spring Sunday in May.

With the soup pan on the boil, lots of lettuce to rinse and transform into plates of salad, with buns needing to go in the oven and the cups having just run out, it can be difficult even for me to say straight off which cakes don't contain nuts, hazelnut oil or almond paste.

I have to rush in to fetch my big black file, which is covered in dough and flour, and flip backwards and forwards with the questions whizzing about my ears. Finally the grateful guest has got an answer and chosen their nutless cake, and I swear for the thousandth time never ever again to bake a cake that has the slightest thing to do with nuts!

Pistachio and chocolate tart.

## T-bread

*T-bread is almond slices, made using almond paste for its lovely flavour. They are filled with blueberry-and-raspberry jam, preferably home-made.*

*Cake:*
600 g almond paste
2 egg whites

*Filling:*
About 1 dl blueberry-and-raspberry jam

• Grate the almond paste coarsely and mix it with the egg whites.
• Shape into lengths. Use icing sugar as "flour" if the dough is too sticky. Place the lengths of dough on to a greased baking sheet and flatten them somewhat. Spread with the jam.
• Bake at 175° for 10–15 minutes. Cut the lengths into slanting slices when they have cooled somewhat.

## Almond squares with chocolate and raisins

*(Makes about 15–20)*

*Crisp and tasty squares with a distinct taste of butter and chocolate.*

260 g butter
2 dl sugar
2 tsp vanilla sugar
5 dl flour
200 g almonds
200 g dark Belgian cooking chocolate
100 g raisins

• Cream together the butter and sugar until white and porous. Add the flour.
• Blanch the almonds and chop them quite finely. Coarsely chop the chocolate. Fold the almonds, chocolate and raisins into the dough, which should become a bit crumbly.
• Press out the dough in a greased roasting pan.
• Bake at 175° for 20–25 minutes. Cut up into fairly large squares when the cake has cooled somewhat.

## Coconut tops with chocolate and orange

*Chocolate and candied orange peel give these otherwise ordinary coconut tops a new taste.*

50 g butter
2 eggs
1 1/2 dl sugar
7 dl coconut
3–5 tbsp candied orange peel
100 g roughly chopped cooking chocolate

• Melt the butter and allow to cool.
• Whisk the egg and sugar until light and fluffy.
• Mix in the other ingredients and leave the mixture to swell for about 10–15 minutes.
• Shape the coconut tops and place them on a greased baking sheet.
• Bake at 160° for about 12–15 minutes.

## Nut tops

*(Makes about 25)*

*A classic! A bit chewy with a distinct hazelnut flavour. Let a whole kernel decorate each cake and proclaim its contents.*

2 1/2 dl hazelnut kernels
2 1/2 dl icing sugar
3 egg whites

*For decoration:*
About 25 hazelnut kernels

• Finely grind the hazelnuts and mix them with the icing sugar.
• Whisk the egg whites until stiff. Carefully stir in the nut-and-sugar mixture.
• Drop the cakes onto a greased baking sheet. Press a hazelnut kernel into each cake.
• Bake at 180° for 10–15 minutes.

## Siena cakes

*(Makes about 25)*

*Siena is a little town in Italy which is famous for its almond cakes. These ones are not real Siena cakes but they are very good anyway.*

200 g almond
3 1/2 dl icing sugar
2 egg whites
75 g candied orange peel

• Blanch the almonds and grind them finely.
• Whisk the egg whites into stiff foam.
• Carefully mix all the ingredients. Leave the mixture for about 10 minutes.
• Drop the cakes onto greased baking sheets.
• Bake at 175° for 10–15 minutes. Powder the cakes with a little icing sugar before serving.

## Almond cakes

*(Makes about 25)*

300 g almonds
2 1/2 dl sugar
3 egg whites

*For decoration:*
About 25 almonds

Simakaka

Pudersockret och mandelns sötma
blandar sig med den bittra
smaken från apelsinskal.
Det vita florfunna pudret
sprider sig som en sky över min
svarta klänning ner i mitt
knä, medan jag ser ut över
trädgården i Rosendal ...

Krukmakare
Ingegerd Råman

• Blanch the almonds and grate finely, then mix them with the sugar.
• Whisk the egg whites until stiff. Fold into the almond mixture.
• Drop the cakes onto greased baking plates and decorate with an almond in each cake.
• Bake at 175° for 12–15 minutes.

## Almond moulds with cloudberry jam and cream
*(Makes about 40)*

*Making almond moulds is always a bit fiddly. This makes it an excellent rainy day occupation for us at the Rosendal café. With lots of fingers helping, the work is done quickly and easily and gives us enough almond moulds for a whole sunny Sunday.*

2 dl almonds
200 g butter
1 1/2 dl sugar
1 egg
4 dl flour

*For serving:*
Whipped cream and cloudberry jam

• Grate the almonds finely.
• Cream together the butter and sugar until white and porous.
• Add the egg, almond and flour. Knead the dough well and leave in a cold place for a couple of hours.
• Grease small pleated forms and press the dough into them.
• Bake the moulds at 200° for about 8 minutes.
• Fill them with a blob of cream and a little cloudberry jam.

## Nut roll with coffee cream
*A nut swiss roll filled with coffee-flavoured buttercream. Tastes best served cold.*

*Cake:*
3 eggs
1 1/2 dl sugar
1 1/2 dl hazelnuts
1 1/2 tbsp potato flour
1 1/2 tsp baking powder

*Filling:*
150 g butter
2 dl icing sugar
2 tsp vanilla sugar
1–2 tbsp cocoa
2 tsp instant coffee powder
1 egg yolk

*Cake:*
• Whisk the egg and sugar until white and fluffy.
• Grind the nuts and mix them into the flour, together with the baking powder.
• Spread the mixture onto greaseproof paper in a roasting pan.
• Bake the cake at 225° for 5 minutes.
• Sprinkle the cake with a little sugar. Put a sheet of greaseproof paper on top and turn it over with the help of a baking sheet. Remove the other paper.

*Filling:*
• Cream together the butter and icing sugar. Add cocoa, vanilla sugar and coffee powder. Finally stir in the egg yolk.
• Spread the mixture on the cake when cool and roll it up from the long side. Leave it in a cold place for a while before serving.

## Coconut cake with coffee glazing
*Cake:*
2 eggs
2 dl sugar
100g butter
1 dl water
1 1/2 dl coconut
2 1/2 dl flour
1 1/2 tsp baking powder

*Glaze:*
1 1/2 dl double cream
1 1/2 dl sugar
1 tbsp butter
1–2 tsp instant coffee powder

*Cake:*
• Whisk the egg and sugar until white and fluffy.
• Melt the butter and add the water. Leave to cool somewhat.
• Mix all the ingredients into the egg-and-sugar mixture. Stir well. Pour the mixture into a greased and cocoa-sprinkled tin (about 23 cm in diameter).
• Bake the cake at 180° for about 30 minutes.

*Glaze:*
• Boil the cream, sugar and butter for about 25 minutes or until the sauce has thickened somewhat. Add the coffee powder and let the glaze cool before it is spread over the cake. Whipped cream goes well with this cake.

## Pistachio and chocolate tart
*This tart has a delicious clash of flavours, between the salty pistachio nuts and the sweet-sour orange chocolate. The tart also looks terrific, with the green pistachio nuts in the brown filling. Serve with whipped cream. (Continued on page 101.)*

Almond moulds, nut roll with coffee cream, almond squares with chocolate and raisins, pistachio and chocolate tart, coconut tops with chocolate and orange, t-bread, nut tart, Siena cake and coconut cake with coffee glazing.

## WALNUT BREAD

*This is a good bread to serve with soup or a salad.*
*It is one of the kinds that we bake for the shop*
*every day.*

50 g fresh yeast
6 dl water
2 tsp sugar
1/2 tbsp salt
About 1 1/3 l flour
3 1/2 dl walnuts

*For glazing:*
1 egg

• Dissolve the yeast in the lukewarm water.
• Add the sugar, salt and 1 litre of the flour. Mix
well.
• Coarsely chop the walnuts and add them to the
dough. Mix in a little more flour. Knead the dough
until supple and shiny. Leave to rise under a cloth
for about 45 minutes.
• Knead the dough again. Shape into two loaves and
leave to rise without a cloth for about 15 minutes.
Brush the loaves with egg.
• Bake the walnut bread at 225° for about 20
minutes.

*Tart:*
125 g butter
3 dl flour
2 tbsp cold water
2 tbsp icing sugar

*Filling:*
100 g shelled pistachio nuts
Juice and peel of 2 oranges
50 g butter
75 g dark Belgian cooking chocolate
1 dl sugar
1/2 dl golden syrup
3 eggs
1/2 dl double cream

*Tart:*
• Chop together all the ingredients for the pastry and leave in a cold place for about an hour.
• Roll out the pastry and line a detachable baking ring (about 23 cm in diameter). Prick the bottom and cover the edge with aluminium foil. Bake blind at 200° for about 10 minutes.

*Filling:*
• Shell the pistachio nuts. Grate the orange peel and squeeze out the juice.
• Melt the butter in a saucepan and add the chocolate. Stir until it has all melted. Mix in all the ingredients except the pistachio nuts.
• Pour the filling into the tart case and sprinkle with lots of nuts.
• Bake at 175° for about 35 minutes.

# Nut tart

*Anyone who loves nuts will find this tart irresistible. It's packed with nuts in a somewhat chewy filling, and it really lives up to its name. The nut tart needs some whipped cream to really be at its best.*

*Tart:*
Puff pastry. See apple strudel page 42. You can, of course, use frozen puff pastry.

*Filling:*
3 eggs
1 dl golden syrup
3/4 dl demerara sugar
2 tbsp vanilla sugar
100 g butter, at room temperature
100 g walnuts
100 g hazelnuts
75 g almonds

*Tart:*
• Roll out the puff pastry and line a baking ring (about 23 cm in diameter). Prick the bottom and cover the edge with aluminium foil.
• Bake blind at 200° for 10 minutes.

*Filling:*
• Whisk the egg, syrup, demerara sugar and vanilla sugar until fluffy. Add the soft butter, in thin slices.
• Chop the nuts very coarsely and mix them into the egg mixture. Pour the filling into the tart case.
• Bake the tart at 175° for about 30 minutes.

Nut tops.

Herbs & Spices

When we talk of spices, we can mean very different things. It is very difficult to define what are spices and what are herbs, since the word spice in its original meaning is quite simply herb. For me, it feels as if spices are those exotic kinds that we can't grow on our latitudes, whilst those that we can grow are herbs, sometimes known as herbal spices. There are always exceptions, and as I say, this definition suits me, but for someone else maybe all spices are herbs or vice versa.

Even with such a simple categorisation it is difficult to define what exactly a spice is. There is no common botanical origin: cinnamon comes from the bark of a tree, saffron from a flower and ginger from a root. It is easier to give a description of herbs, where in most cases we use the leaves.

Spices and herbs are used for different reasons. Sometimes to enhance an already existing flavour and sometimes quite simply to provide flavour. I use them more and more as a way of giving soul or character to a dish or something I have baked. At the Rosendal café it is usual that we sprinkle lots of lemon balm leaves over a lemon cake or lots of basil over a feta cheese salad. During the months that we can pick them in the garden, edible flowers can add further poetry to the table. It's such fun and so easy to decorate a plate or compose a buffet table using whatever fresh herbs or edible flowers are available on that particular day.

People in Scandinavia are used to spicing their cakes and pastries at Christmas time. But for me it has become both a natural thing, and a challenge, to use spices in my baking all the year round. Sometimes the results are not so good, but occasionally it can give rise to a fantastic taste combination. The salty-sweet little almond rusks in this chapter are one of my more successful experiments.

It is rewarding to bake bread with spices or herbs in it. You can give bread a wonderful green tinge and a fuller flavour if you add lots of herbs, for example basil or parsley. You can taste this most distinctly in our herb bread.

Rosemary is well known for flavouring lamb. Therefore you might think it a bit strange to use rosemary in flavouring our fruit fingers, but they are a must to taste! Fruit fingers are very popular and they are sold by the bag or individually in the garden shop. Thyme is another typical savoury herb that does itself justice in our thyme rusks.

At Rosendal we also flavour both refined sugar and demerara sugar with various spices. We leave the sugar to absorb the flavour for a few weeks in glass jars on a shelf in the kitchen. Usually we use well-planned flavourings, but sometimes we like to try more adventurous combinations.

The glass jars give our kitchen a special atmosphere, and also make it easy for us to try out new flavourings for both baking and jam making. So just keep on spicing!

Spiced vinegar. *Previous page:* small salty twist buns. *Page 109:* salty-sweet almond rusks, ginger cakes, cardamom cakes, cardamom rusks, rosemary flavoured fruit fingers and thyme rusks.

## Salty-sweet almond rusks

*(Makes about 25–30)*

*Tiny cakes that makes you want more. They are perfect as a snack with drinks. They are salty and sweet at the same time.*

100 g almonds
1 egg white
1 2/3 dl icing sugar
3–4 tsp salt

- Blanch the almonds and grind finely.
- Vigorously whisk the egg white.
- Mix all the ingredients and add salt to taste. Leave the mixture for about 15 minutes.
- Drop out small rusks with a spoon.
- Bake at 175° for 8–10 minutes.

## Ginger biscuits

*(Makes about 30)*

*Small crunchy biscuits that sell like hot cakes in our shop.*

1 1/2 dl golden syrup
5 tsp ground ginger
1 tsp bicarbonate
125 g butter
4 dl whole wheat flour
2 dl flour
2 1/2 dl demerara sugar
2 tsp baking powder

- Heat the syrup in a saucepan. Mix in the ginger and bicarbonate.
- Rub the butter and the flour into a grainy mass. Add sugar and baking powder.
- Mix the ginger mixture with the flour mixture and work into a soft dough.
- Roll pieces of dough into small balls and put them on a greased baking plate. Flatten them a little.
- Bake the biscuits at 200° for about 15 minutes.

## Small salty twist buns

*(Makes about 25–30)*

*Coffee is perhaps not the best thing to have with salty pastries. They need something cooling, for example a glass of beer or wine. Our own spiced salt gives these small twist buns a green nuance.*

75 g butter
3 tbsp double cream
2 dl flour
1 tsp salt

*For glazing:*
Water and spiced salt

- Cream the butter. Add the cream, salt and flour. Work into a supple dough.
- Roll out short lengths (about 6 cm long) and shape into small twists.
- Brush the twists with water and dip them in the spiced salt. Place on a greased baking sheet and lightly flatten them.
- Bake the twists at 175° for about 8–10 minutes.

## Cardamom rusks

*(Makes about 25)*

*These rusks are easy to bake, pretty and delicate. They have a fine flavour of newly crushed cardamom. We sell them by the hecto in brown, plain paper bags in our garden shop.*

125 g butter
1/2 dl sugar
1 egg
3 dl porridge oats (oat meal)
3 dl flour
Scant 2 tsp baking powder
4 tsp freshly crushed cardamom kernels
1 1/2 dl milk

- Cream the butter and the sugar until white and porous. Add the egg.
- Stir together the oats, flour, baking powder and crushed cardamom. Add this to the mixture, alternately with the milk.
- Shape into two lengths and place them on a greased baking sheet.
- Bake the lengths at 200° for about 20 minutes.
- Cut them in diagonal slices. Dry the rusks at 100° for about 40–60 minutes until they are completely dry.

## Thyme rusks

*(Makes about 45–50)*

120 g almonds
2 eggs
2 dl sugar
2 tbsp freshly crushed dried thyme (the sugar and thyme can be replaced by thyme sugar)
1 tsp salt
5–6 dl flour
1 tsp baking powder
100 g dark Belgian cooking chocolate, coarsely chopped

*For glazing:*
Egg white

- Finely grind a third of the almonds and chop the rest *very* coarsely. (*Continued on page* 108.)

# Herb bread
*(1 large or 2 small loaves)*

*This bread is like no other. Wild and beautiful, its place is beside the soup pot. It is very popular and its little green speckles invite many questions from our guests. They are pleased when they hear that they are basil and parsley.*

50 g butter
2 dl milk
50 g fresh yeast
3/4 dl golden syrup
2 tsp salt
200 g cottage cheese
5 tbsp fresh chopped basil
5 tbsp fresh chopped parsley
4 dl whole wheat flour
About 7 dl flour

*For glazing and decoration:*
1 egg
Coarse salt

• Melt the butter and mix it with the milk. Heat to lukewarm.
• Dissolve the yeast in the liquid. Add syrup, salt, cottage cheese and the herbs. Mix well. Stir in all the whole wheat flour and the other flour a little at a time. Knead the dough until supple but still quite moist. Leave to rise under a cloth for 45 minutes.
• Knead the dough again. Make one large or two small loaves and place on a greased baking sheet. Leave to rise for 20 minutes.
• Brush the bread with egg and, if you wish, sprinkle with some coarse salt. Put it in an oven at 200°, but immediately lower the temperature to 175°.
• Bake the bread for about 20–25 minutes, until it sounds hollow when you tap underneath. Leave to cool under a cloth.

• Mix the almond, eggs, salt, sugar and thyme (or thymesugar). Add 3 dl of the flour mixed with baking powder and then the lightly floured chocolate. Finally mix in the rest of the flour, a little at a time, making sure not to use too much.
• Roll out into lengths and place them on greased baking sheets. Brush the lengths with egg white.
• Bake at 180° for about 15–20 minutes.
• Slice the lengths into rusks and dry them at 100° for about 30 minutes.

## Rosemary-flavoured fruit fingers
*(Makes about 20)*

*Everyone who has been to the Mediterranean countries has smelt that characteristic scent from wild rosemary. Using rosemary as a spice for baking sweet things can seem a bit strange, but in these fruit fingers the result is extraordinarily good!*

2 eggs
2 dl brown sugar
1 tbsp vanilla sugar
4 dl raisins
150 g sunflower seed kernels
1–2 tbsp dried rosemary
1/2 tsp salt
1 tsp baking powder
About 2 1/2 dl flour

• Whisk the eggs, brown sugar and vanilla sugar until fluffy. Add the raisins and sunflower seed kernels.
• Crush the rosemary in a mortar and mix it with the salt, baking powder and flour. Stir into the egg mixture. Spread out the mixture into a well greased roasting pan.
• Bake the cake at about 200° for 25–30 minutes. Cut it into 2 cm wide and 5 cm long "fingers".

## Cardamom cake

200 g butter
2 1/2 dl sugar
3 eggs
About 4 1/2 dl flour
1 tsp baking powder
1 tbsp newly crushed cardamom
Scant 1 dl double cream

• Cream the butter and the sugar until white and porous. Add the eggs one at a time.
• Stir the baking powder and the cardamom into the flour and add to the egg-sugar mixture, alternately with the cream.
• Pour the mixture into a greased and breadcrumbed round cake tin of about 1 1/2–2 litres. Do not smooth the surface. It is more beautiful if uneven.
• Bake the cake at 175° for about 40 minutes. Turn off the oven and leave for about 15 minutes.

Ginger pears and preserved ginger with lemon grass.

## Ginger pears
*Ginger pears are a classic dessert. Put into a beautiful glass jar, they make a greatly appreciated present.*

2 kg pears
2 l water
1 3/4 l sugar
5–6 pieces of fresh ginger
1 lemon for lemon water

• Peel the pears but leave the stalks. Put the pears in lemon water so that they do not turn brown.
• Peel and cut the ginger into smallish pieces.
• Boil up the water, sugar and ginger. Stir until the sugar has dissolved. Put in the pears and boil for 15–25 minutes. How long they need to boil depends on the size, ripeness and variety of pear.
• Serve the pears with lightly whipped cream or ice cream. If you are going to eat them later, conserve in glass jars. See page 213.

## Spiced sugar
*Spiced sugar is excellent to use in baking, for jam making and in savoury dishes where you dare to put in a little sugar. Try different flavourings and demerara sugar occasionally if you wish.*

## Thyme sugar
*Layer dried thyme and sugar in a glass jar. Put on the lid and leave the sugar to stand for at least two weeks. Then you can use it just like ordinary sugar, with spices and all.*

Fårö 11.5.84.

Kära Monica!

Du måste ~~allihopa~~ ile se att jag ~~ila~~
skriva något om ~~sunkbron~~ ~~...~~ ...
... blå ... Gåda ... ... ... Jag
... i ... ... ... alltjämt ... ...
... Fem ... ... ... jag ...
... ... ... sju ... ...
... surr ... eld ... ... klädde ...
... band ... ... Island ... ...
... jag ... ... ... ...
i ... ... finns en ...
... ... röd av ... i ...
... ... ...
... det är ... ... ...
... ... ... på ... som

Norra ... sig. Ja, det är ...
... ... men jag ...
... : ... ...
... ... ...
på ... ... paradiset ...
... ... Jag vet inte riktigt
... jag ... ... det ..., det låter väl
ALLT FÖR ... slaget, men jag ... ...
... andra ord så ...

Kära hälsningar
Jerum.

Vegetables

Most people have their own special relationship with vegetables. They either adore vegetables or they hate them. Some people see them as a necessary evil that you have to force yourself to eat a couple of times a week. My mother-in-law Annie never eats a vegetable without pointing out that she is eating some "grass" for the sake of the vitamins. She calls all vegetables grass and doesn't really like eating any at all. To get her to understand that we have guests that come here every day to eat our salads – mozzarella, tomatoes and basil, feta cheese salad, salmon salad or whatever – is impossible. Then, when I mention that some people are in fact addicted to a slice of carrot cake twice a week or think that nothing is more exciting than our zucchini cake; she is completely at a loss.

When a café like ours is part of a garden where our own vegetables are grown, it is easy to be tempted into using them in just about everything. The ones which aren't used for the meal of the day or sold in the garden shop, are used in baking or in different kinds of preserves. It is also an experience for our visitors to see the vegetables germinate, grow and be harvested, and then to see them dressed for the shop or made into cakes and preserves. Nothing is allowed to go to waste. The bits that for some reason can't be used, go back to the soil as compost.

Potato cake with chocolate.

# Zucchini cake
*(Two baking tins of about 1 1/2 litres)*

*A moist cake that keeps well. It looks just like an ordinary ginger cake.*

2 dl sunflower oil or other oil with neutral taste
4 dl brown sugar
4 dl finely grated zucchini (courgette)
4 eggs
About 7–8 dl flour
1 tsp baking powder
1 tsp bicarbonate
2 tsp cinnamon
1 tsp salt
3/4 dl crème fraiche
1 1/2 dl coarsely chopped walnuts

• Whisk the oil and the sugar. Add the zucchini and the eggs, one at a time.
• Stir together flour, baking powder, bicarbonate, cinnamon and salt. Add the mixture alternately with the crème fraiche.
• Finally fold in the walnuts. Use a little more flour if necessary. (The amount of flour varies according to the liquid content of the zucchini.)
• Pour the mixture into two greased and breadcrumbed baking tins of about 1 1/2 litres.
• Bake the cakes at 175° for 60 minutes on the bottom rung of the oven.

# Potato cake with chocolate
*A cake completely without flour! It tastes best if it is still a bit sticky when it has been baked. Whipped cream goes very well with this cake.*

3–4 medium sized potatoes
100 g butter
2 eggs
1 dl sugar
1 tbsp vanilla sugar
5 tbsp cocoa
1/2 tsp salt

*For decoration:*
Icing sugar

• Peel, boil and press the potatoes.
• Melt the butter and mix in all the ingredients.
• Pour out the mixture into a greased and breadcrumbed cake tin (about 18 cm in diameter).
• Bake the cake at about 150° for 30–40 minutes. Powder with icing sugar.

# Carrot cake
*A favourite at Rosendal. Tasty, moist and filling.*

*Cake:*
2 1/2 dl sunflower oil or other oil with neutral taste
3 1/2 dl sugar
4 dl carrots, grated finely
3 eggs
4 dl flour
1 tsp baking powder
1 tsp bicarbonate
1/2 tsp salt
1/2 tsp freshly grated nutmeg
1 tsp cinnamon
1/2–1 dl very coarsely chopped walnuts

*Topping:*
200 g melted butter, cooled
200 g Philadelphia cheese
3 dl icing sugar
2 tsp vanilla sugar
Juice and peel of 1 lemon

*Cake:*
• Whisk sugar and oil until white. Add the grated carrots and then the eggs, one at a time. Mix together the other dry ingredients and stir them into the mixture. Finally add the walnuts.
• Pour the mixture into a greased and breadcrumbed cake tin (about 23 cm in diameter).
• Bake the cake at 200° for about 40–45 minutes.

*Topping:*
• When the cake has cooled, whisk all the ingredients into a fluffy cream and spread over the cake.
• Leave the cake in a cold place for a while until the topping has set somewhat.

# Carrot bread with thyme
*Bread that has the slightly sweet taste of carrots and the delightful scent of thyme. Can be served with hot soup.*

50 g butter
50 g fresh yeast
2 1/2 dl milk
2 1/2 dl water
2 tbsp golden syrup
1 tbsp salt
2 tbsp freshly chopped thyme, or 1 tbsp dried
3 1/2 dl grated carrots
5 dl whole wheat flour
8–9 dl flour

*For glaze and decoration:*
1 egg
Sea salt and thyme

- Melt the butter. Mix in the milk and the water.
- Dissolve the yeast in some of the lukewarm liquid.
- Add the syrup, salt, thyme, carrots, whole wheat flour and finally the flour, a little at a time.
- Mix carefully and knead well. Leave to rise under a cloth for about 45 minutes.
- Turn out the dough and knead it for a few minutes. Shape into long loaves or round buns.
- Leave to rise without a cloth on a greased baking sheet for about 15 minutes.
- Brush the bread with the lightly beaten egg and sprinkle with a little sea salt and thyme.
- Bake the buns (about 20) at 250° for about 12 minutes. Long loaves should be baked at 200–225° for about 17–20 minutes.

# Bread with sun-dried tomatoes, onions and olives

*One of my own favourites. This bread has a continental taste.*

50 g fresh yeast
4 1/2 dl water
1/2 dl olive oil
3 tbsp sugar
1 tbsp salt
1 small onion, finely chopped
75 g "sun-dried" tomatoes (see page 161)
20 black olives, pitted
1/2 red pepper
1/2 yellow pepper
1/2 green pepper
1,1–1,3 l flour

*For glazing and decoration:*
Olive oil and coarse salt

- Dissolve the yeast in the lukewarm water. Mix in the olive oil and sugar. Leave to stand for about 10 minutes.
- Meanwhile chop the onion, tomatoes, peppers and olives.
- Add the flour (the lesser amount), salt and vegetables to the liquid.
- Knead the dough well and shape into a round bun. Brush it with olive oil and leave to rise for 1 1/2 hours.
- Turn out the dough and knead vigorously. Shape into two loaves.
- Slash the bread and brush with oil. Sprinkle with a little flour and coarse salt.
- Bake at 200° for 35—40 minutes.

Bread with sun-dried tomatoes, onion and olives. *Opposite page:* carrot cake and carrot bread with thyme.

# Vegen til lykken

Vise til Monika                                    fra Yngve Gåsøy

Lenge trodde jeg meg vite at lykken
var en sang om liv og lyst og kjærlig-
-het, ja liv i lystelige sprang. Men
tross iherdig leting jeg lykken aldrig
fann. Til Rosendals café jeg dro, og
angsten, den forsvann. Hun stod der stolt i pakgir-
-akt, med dagg på ganne nese hals, og rakte fram sitt bakverk
-prakt. Hjertet slog opp til en vals. Det
stod da plutselig klart for meg hvor feil jeg hadde
hatt, Ty. lykken er en Morots-kjærta
Mo - nika har skapt.

a - 4

Seeds & Flowers

Using seeds and flowers in the bakery and kitchen is both fun and exciting. Fun, because it's easy to create a ravishingly beautiful dish with the help of edible flowers. Exciting because there are so many possibilities and the taste combinations can sometimes be really terrific. Let your imagination loose!

We use flowers every day to decorate our bakery produce at the garden café. Light blue borage reposes on the carrot cake, whilst red or yellow nasturtiums spread out over the dark brown chocolate cake. The zucchini flowers on the zucchini cake emphasise how close the garden is to the bakery. By adding blue-violet chive flowers to a plain salad you can enhance the simplest meal. An avocado salad decorated with yellow, orange and red nasturtiums can inspire anyone to start cultivating their own nasturtium bed. Adding dried flowers or petals to dough is always an adventure. The bread is given a beautiful colour and its own special flavour, depending on the kind of flowers you have used.

Rose leaf marmalade is just as wonderfully romantic and delicious as the name suggests. Yes, there are lots of edible flowers that the garden can give the kitchen, and with their help you can enhance the poetry of your cuisine. So don't be afraid of taking violets, daisies or marigold petals into the kitchen.

Poppyseeds are mostly used as decoration on pale-coloured bread. They have no smell but have a good, characteristic taste. I use them as a main ingredient in our poppy cake or as a filling for our poppy long-buns. Sometimes I quite simply sprinkle a greased cake tin, meant for a dark brown chocolate cake, with these tiny dark blue seeds. They add a wonderful flavour and make a beautiful cake.

One of my favourites is poppyseeds that have been added to melted butter and poured over lightly cooked spring vegetables. Probably the easiest way to use poppyseeds is to add a decilitre or so to ordinary pastry and then fill the tart case with lots of beautiful red berries. Finally, I can reveal that there are 900 000 poppyseeds in a kilo, so you only need about 100 000 or so to add a personal flourish to your baking!

Sunflower seed bread.

Lavender rusks and lavender sugar.

Poppyseed cake and poppy long-bun.

# Lavender rusks

*When we bake lavender rusks, a scent that reminds you of Provence spreads throughout Rosendal. The lavender flowers give the rusks beautiful blue speckles.*

120 g almonds
2 eggs
2 dl lavender sugar (se page 126)
1 tsp salt
About 5–6 dl flour
1 tsp baking powder
100 g dark Belgian cooking chocolate, roughly chopped

*For glazing:*
1 egg white

• Grate finely a third of the almonds and chop the rest *very* roughly.
• Mix the almonds, egg, sugar and salt. Add 3 dl of the flour mixed with the baking powder, and then the lightly floured chocolate. Finally mix in the rest of the flour, a little at a time. Make sure not to use too much.
• Roll out lengths of dough and put them on a greased baking sheet. Brush them with egg white.
• Bake at 180° for about 15–20 minutes.
• Cut the lengths into rusks and dry them at 100° for about 30–40 minutes.

# Poppyseed cake

*A somewhat unusual cake. Its blue spots gives it an interesting appearance.*

100 g poppyseeds
2 dl milk
2 eggs
2 dl demerara sugar
1 1/2 dl hazelnut or almond oil. (Note: you can't substitute these with olive or sunflower oil. It changes the taste too much.)
1 1/2 dl whole wheat flour
Scant 2 1/2 dl flour
2 tsp baking powder
2 tsp cinnamon

• Put 50 g poppyseeds to soak in the milk for one hour.
• Whisk the egg and the demerara sugar until fluffy. Whisk in the oil slowly.
• Fold in the other ingredients, but save a couple of tablespoons of poppyseeds.
• Pour the mixture into a greased and breadcrumbed cake tin of about 1 1/2 litres. Sprinkle over the rest of the poppyseeds.
• Bake the cake at 200° for about 25–30 minutes.

# Poppy long-bun

*This cake gets its name from the attractive and somewhat unusual filling. For the dough, see Mother's long-bun, page 91.*

*Filling:*
1 1/2 dl blue poppyseeds
2 tbsp butter
1/2 dl sugar
1/2 dl milk

*For glazing:*
1 egg and poppyseeds

• Crush the poppyseeds in a mortar.
• Melt the butter in a saucepan and stir in the sugar. Add the poppyseeds and the milk. Let the mixture simmer on a low heat for 5–10 minutes. Remove from the heat and leave to cool.
• Roll out the dough (which has already been left to rise) into a rectangle. Spread the filling on the dough and roll it up like a swiss roll. Place the roll on a greased baking sheet and cut flaps in the dough with a sharp knife. Fold the flaps alternately to the right and to the left.
• Brush the lengths with egg and sprinkle with poppyseeds.
• Bake at 225° for 20-25 minutes.

# Sunflower seed bread

*(Makes about 20)*
*I bake bread every day for the shop. The assortment varies from day to day. Baguettes, large loaves and small rolls spread their fragrance every morning at 11 o'clock, when the garden shop opens. These sunflower seed loaves are very popular, there are seldom any left over.*

7 dl water
50 g fresh yeast
3 dl sunflower seed kernels
6 dl porridge oats (oat meal)
2 tsp herbal salt
About 1 1/5 l flour

*For glazing:*
1 egg
3 tsp herbal salt
About 1 dl sunflower seed kernels

• Dissolve the yeast in the lukewarm water.
• Add the sunflower seeds and the oats. Stir well and leave for about 5 minutes.
• Mix in the herbal salt and the flour, a little at a time. Thoroughly knead into a supple dough.
• Leave to rise under a cloth for 45 minutes.
• Knead the dough again and shape into round buns that are placed on a greased and lightly floured baking sheet.

• Leave the buns to rise without a cloth for about 15 minutes.
• Brush them with the whisked egg mixed with herbal salt and sprinkle with sunflower seed kernels.
• Bake the buns at 250° for about 12–15 minutes.

## Sesame baguettes
*(Makes about 3–4)*

50 g fresh yeast
6 dl water
1/2 tbsp sugar
1/2 tbsp salt
Scant 1 dl sesame seeds
4 dl whole wheat flour
About 1 l flour

*For glazing:*
1 egg and sesame seeds

• Dissolve the yeast in the lukewarm water.
• Add the sugar, salt and sesame seeds. Stir well. Mix in the flour and whole wheat flour, a little at a time. Knead thoroughly until the dough is supple.
• Leave to rise under a cloth for 45 minutes.
• Knead the dough again and shape into baguettes. Make diagonal slashes with a sharp knife. Leave to rise for 15–20 minutes.
• Brush the baguettes with egg and sprinkle with sesame seeds.
• Bake at 225° for about 20 minutes.

## Elderberry sorbet
*Sorbet is a refreshing summer dessert. Since we have our own elderberry tree in the garden we usually make it with our own elderberry juice.*

4 dl undiluted elderberry juice
Juice of 2 oranges
4 egg whites
1–2 tbsp sugar depending on how sweet the juice is

• Pour the elderberry juice and the orange juice into a shallow dish. Put it in the freezer until semi-frozen.
• Whisk the egg whites into stiff foam. Mix in sugar to taste.
• Mix the whisked egg white with the half-frozen juice. Put the mixture back into the freezer for about 2–3 hours, but take it out occasionally and stir vigorously.
• Decorate with elderberry sprigs when serving.

## Lavender sugar
*Put alternate layers of dried lavender flowers and sugar in a glass jar. Leave to stand for at least two weeks. The sugar can be used like ordinary sugar. Include the small flowers. You can see them clearly in our lavender rusks and they give the rusks a blue nuance.*

Till Monika från
Charlotta Åkerblom,
Café-flicka o
konststuderande
1994

Some of the indefatigable café staff with Per Frisk (our accountant), Malin Löfstrand (master gardener) and Thommy
Berggren: Sofie Sundin, Per Frisk & Malin Löfstrand, Katarina Nimmervoll, Josefine Wiklund & Marzena Zuchowska,

Maja Vållberg, Sara Teleman, Kalle Bolldén, Naná de Graaff, Lisa Munthe, Janne Lindström, Karolina Blixt, Elias Sjöberg, Thommy Berggren & Monika Ahlberg, Sofia Tägtström, Sara Jacobsson and Anna Sundström.

Kära Monika;

om ett kök inte luktar vitlök
så är det inte något riktigt kök!
Så brukar en av mina vänner
säga då hon kommer in hos mig.
Då jag smakat Dina saltbakade,
ugnsbakade, storartade vitlökar
lämnade de mig ingen ro förrän
jag själv lagat till dem.
Nu luktar mitt kök ännu stark-
-are (värre, sa' nå'n).
Så sällan en maträtt förenar en
rustikt tilldragande smak med
utseende! man äter för många!
Så – glöm inte den lilla engelska
versen ...
But lest your kissing should
                  be spoil't
Your Onion must be thorough
                  boil'd!
(en vän har översatt så här)
Om kyssen ej ska' gå på tok
lägg löken i ett redigt kok.

              Din vän Hiram

Food, preserves.
Oil & Vinegar

Food is tradition and culture. The culture of food varies according to where you are in the world, or the availability of ingredients, or inspiration. Just think of Tuscany in Italy, with its beautiful and aromatic landscape, which has a long culinary tradition stretching from the days of the Etruscans. It is simple food, but imaginative at the same time. I am immensely influenced by Italian cuisine! My kitchen also happens to be in a beautiful and abundant garden, with every possibility of growing everything for our daily needs. That makes it easy to serve wholesome food made with personality, to create imaginative preserves, or to pick a herbal bouquet to decorate beautiful jars filled with oil or vinegar. If you then keep the jars and bottles on a shelf, you create a warm and inviting atmosphere in the kitchen. All this is simple and we can all do it in our own homes. Surely a lovely kitchen is the best place for convivial company. Everyone feels at home there!

Open sandwiches: ham salad, Brie cheese and tomato & onion. *Following page:* marinated sugar peas and carrot slants.

## Sandwiches at the garden café

*We serve a number of different open sandwiches at the café. Besides our usual kinds with cheese and ham, we have some that are a bit more exciting. I've chosen four different ones that are tasty and easy to make:*

*Tomato and onion:*
Light bread, butter
Lettuce
Slices of tomato and onion
Herbal salt and freshly ground black pepper
Parsley

• Butter a slice of light bread, put on a lettuce leaf and some generous slices of tomato and onion. Finally sprinkle with a little herbal salt and black pepper. Decorate with lots of parsley.

*Brie on dark bread:*
Butter, lettuce
French Brie cheese
Celery
Parsley
Olives
Sun-dried tomatoes

• Butter a slice of dark bread, put on a lettuce leaf, a thick slice of Brie cheese, a piece of celery, a few olives, parsley and finally a sun-dried tomato.

*Ham salad:*
Dark bread, butter, lettuce
Ham
Estonian lactic-pickled gherkin
Olives
Parsley
Ham salad mix (some chopped ham, finely chopped apple, finely grated celeriac, finely sliced leek, capers, Dijon mustard, equal amounts of mayonnaise and crème fraiche, salt and freshly ground black pepper.

• Butter a slice of dark bread, put on a lettuce leaf, a slice of ham, a large dollop of ham salad mix, and Estonian gherkin, olives and parsley.

*Egg and roe:*
Dark bread
Butter, lettuce
Hard-boiled egg
Lemon wedges
A sprig of dill
Roe mix (crème fraiche, finely chopped onion, whitefish roe or red caviar, finely chopped dill, lemon juice, salt and some freshly ground pepper).

• Butter a slice of dark bread, put on a lettuce leaf, a sliced egg, a generous blob of roe mix, a wedge of lemon and a sprig of dill.

## Oven-baked fresh garlic

*Fresh garlic baked in the oven on a bed of coarse salt is a taste sensation. It is mild, smooth and made juicy by a large knob of butter flavoured with fresh thyme. You can't use dried garlic instead of fresh garlic.*

Coarse salt to cover the tin
5–6 fresh garlic bulbs
About 100 g butter
5 tbsp fresh thyme, chopped

• Spread the salt out in the tin in which the garlic will be baked.
• Remove the outside peel from the whole garlic, but leave the peel on each individual clove. Cut the bulb into halves or quarters.
• Mix the butter and the thyme. Place the garlic on a bed of salt and put a knob of butter on each.
• Bake at 200° for about 20 minutes.

## Small pastry moons with spinach and goat cheese

*(Makes about 10–12)*

*A bit fiddly, but always a success. Serve these small moons as a snack for drinks, or as part of a buffet.*

2–3 pieces of frozen puff pastry
About 50 g butter
About 3 hg fresh spinach, chopped
100 g goat's milk cheese (or feta cheese)
2–3 tbsp fresh basil, chopped
2–4 tbsp double cream

*For glazing:*
1 egg

• Defrost the puff pastry. Use a glass to make rounds. "Stretch" each round somewhat.
• Melt the butter and add the spinach. Stir in the cheese in small pieces, with the basil and the cream. Leave to simmer until thickened.
• Drop a small blob on one half one each round. Fold it into a "moon". Press the edges together firmly with a fork. Put the moons on greaseproof paper on baking sheets and brush them with egg.
• Bake the pastry moons at 200° for about 5–10 minutes.

# Bruschetta

*(About 8–10 servings)*

*Bruschetta is perfect for serving with a drink before a dinner or buffet. When a group arrives at Rosendal for a buffet, I always serve a drink in the apple orchard. I serve something exciting and tasty with the drink. Bruschetta is one of my favourites.*

5 tomatoes
4–5 cloves garlic
5 tbsp fresh, chopped basil
Salt and freshly ground black pepper
1 baguette
Extra virgin olive oil and extra garlic and basil

- Cut up the tomatoes into quite small cubes.
- Finely chop the garlic and fresh basil.
- Mix everything with the chopped tomatoes, salt and pepper to taste. Let the tomato mixture stand at room temperature for at least two hours before serving.
- Divide the baguette lengthways. Brush with olive oil and rub with garlic.
- Grill the bread in the oven for a few minutes. Take out and spread with the tomato mixture. Put back in the oven for another minute. Divide the baguette into suitable pieces and decorate with a basil leaf. Serve immediately!

# Mushroom salad with stock-boiled fennel

*(About 5 servings)*

*Butter, garlic and slices of mushroom spread a delightful scent. The stock-boiled fennel adds an extra flavour. Serve the salad as a starter or as a side dish at a barbecue, for example.*

500 g fresh mushrooms
1 fennel
1 stock cube
75 g butter
3–4 extra virgin olive oil
3–4 cloves of garlic
5 tbsp fresh parsley, chopped
Salt and pepper to taste

- Clean and cut up the mushrooms in fairly thick slices. Rinse and shred the fennel.
- Boil up some water and the stock cube. Boil the shredded fennel for about 4 minutes. Pour off the stock.
- Fry the butter, oil, and finely chopped garlic in a frying pan. Add the mushrooms. Flavour with salt, pepper and half the chopped parsley. Simmer for about 5 minutes. Stir occasionally. Add some more olive oil if it seems dry.
- Mix the mushroom with the lightly boiled fennel. Put on a plate and sprinkle with the remaining parsley.

# Marinated sugar peas and carrot slants

*(About 5 servings)*

*A greatly appreciated and sophisticated side dish at a buffet.*

4 large carrots
150 g sugar peas (mangetout)
1 piece of leek
2 stock cubes
4 tbsp fresh parsley, chopped

*Marinade:*
4 cloves garlic
1/2 dl white wine vinegar
1 1/2 dl extra virgin olive oil
1/2 tbsp dried thyme
1/2 tbsp dried marjoram
Salt and pepper to taste

- Peel the carrots and cut into 3 mm slanting slices. Top and tail the sugar peas if they are fresh. You can also use frozen ones but only add them when there are 2–3 minutes left of the cooking time. Rinse and finely slice the leek into strips.
- Boil up enough water to just cover the vegetables. Add the stock cubes and stir. Boil the vegetables for about 7–8 minutes until they are soft but still firm.
- Pour off the stock.

*Marinade:*
- Blend all the ingredients in a mixer into a thick and rounded sauce. Pour this over the vegetables while they are still hot and stir together. Leave for a few hours to soak up the flavour.
- Arrange the carrots and the sugar peas on a plate. Generously sprinkle with chopped parsley and serve.

# Carrot slants in saffron

*(About 5 servings)*

*Really beautiful! A good side dish for meat or fish.*

4–5 large carrots
A piece of leek
100 g butter
1/2 –1 g saffron
4 tbsp fresh parsley, chopped
1 tbsp marjoram
Salt and freshly ground pepper to taste

- Peel the carrots and cut into 3 mm thick slanting slices. Rinse and slice the leek into strips.
- Boil up enough water to just cover the carrots and leek. Put in the saffron and 50 grams of the butter. Stir. Boil the carrots until soft but still firm. This takes about 7–8 minutes.

• Pour off the water and immediately stir in the remaining 50 grams of the butter so that it melts. Put the carrots on a serving dish, preferably brightly coloured. Sprinkle with the fresh chopped parsley mixed with marjoram. Add a little salt and pepper.

## Deep-fried zucchini flowers

*Serve these flowers as a starter or a side dish at a buffet. You can make them more filling by stuffing them with finely chopped tomato and grated Parmesan cheese before deep-frying. Pick the flowers just before preparation so they do not wither. The long male flowers are the best to use.*

16 newly picked zucchini (courgette) flowers

*Batter:*
2 1/2 dl flour
2 tbsp extra virgin olive oil
5 tbsp finely chopped fresh herbs, e.g. basil, chervil and thyme
1/2 dl white wine
1/2 dl soda water
2 eggs, the yolks and whites separated

*For deep frying:*
8 dl–1 l rapeseed oil or sunflower oil

• Carefully rinse and dry the flowers. Cut off the stem and the green leaves. Remove the stamens and the pistils.

*Batter:*
• Whisk together the flour, oil, spices and egg yolks in a bowl. Add wine and water, stirring continuously, until the batter has as a smooth consistency. Add more water if necessary. Leave to stand for 1/2 hour.
• Whisk the egg whites until stiff and fold them into the batter just before frying.

*Deep frying:*
• Heat up lots of oil. Dip the flowers in the batter and deep-fry them in the oil until golden. Serve immediately with salt and freshly ground pepper.

## Balsamic-marinated artichoke heart.

*Gorgeous hearts in a brown balsamic marinade. The b. sam marinade can be made in greater amounts and kep. in the fridge. It goes very well with salads and lightly boiled spring vegetables.*

1 tin artichoke hearts

*Balsam marinade:*
1 1/2 dl balsamic vinegar
4–5 dl extra virgin olive oil
5–6 garlic cloves
1 tbsp dried thyme
1 tbsp dried chervil
Salt and pepper
Some sprigs of fresh thyme

• Open the tin of artichoke hearts and drain thoroughly.
• Blend all the ingredients for the balsamic marinade in a mixer. Flavour to taste. Pour the marinade over the hearts and toss carefully. Leave to stand for a few hours to marinate. Decorate with fresh sprigs of thyme and serve the hearts as a side dish with meat or smoked fish, on the buffet table, or as a starter with Parma ham and ruccola salad, for example.

## Stuffed iceberg lettuce
*(Makes about 8)*

*Stuffed lettuce leaves with an exciting stuffing. Greatly appreciated when served as a starter, or as a side dish at a buffet.*

1 large head of lettuce (iceberg)
2 mozzarella cheeses (Italian buffalo cheese)
About 1 dl pesto (or red "pesto")
1/2 dl sesame seeds
Olive oil for greasing the dish

• Carefully remove whole leaves from the lettuce. Put them in boiling water for 1/2 minute. Take out and drain well.
• Cut the mozzarella cheese into slices. Put one slice in each lettuce leaf. Spoon a blob of pesto on top. Roll up the leaf into a small packet. Fold in the edges carefully. Put them with the edge downward in a well-oiled ovenproof dish. Sprinkle with sesame seeds.
• Grill at 250° for about 7–10 minutes.

Fresh garlic. *Previous spread:* A. Aubergines with goat cheese and bruschetta. B. Ruccola salad with Parmesan cheese.
C. Balsamic-marinated artichoke hearts. D. Flan with feta cheese, tomato & black olive and stuffed iceberg lettuce. E. Mushroom salad with stock-boiled fennel.
F. Carrot slants in saffron. G. Small pastry moons with spinach and goat's cheese. H. Mixed salad with dandelion leaves.

## Aubergines with goat cheese

*My own variation of the Italian dish aubergine pizzaiola. I use goat's milk cheese from Borgvattnet's dairy, the same cheese that we marinate and conserve in jars. It is really tasty! You can prepare in advance right up until the last heating in the oven.*

1 large aubergine (egg plant)

*For coating and deep-frying:*
Flour and one whisked egg
About 7–8 dl rapeseed oil, you can also use sunflower oil

*Filling:*
About 200 g goat's milk cheese
1/2 dl tomato purée (or red "pesto")
5 tbsp fresh basil, chopped
2 tsp dried oregano
Salt and freshly ground pepper
2–3 tomatoes

• Cut the aubergine in thick slices, about 1–2 cm. Cut a little gash in each slice from the side, to make a little pocket for the filling.
• Turn each slice in the flour and then in the beaten egg.
• Heat the oil in a thick-bottomed saucepan. The temperature is right when a little bit of white bread goes golden brown in a minute or so. Deep-fry the aubergine slices until golden, a few at a time. Take them out and leave to drain.

*Filling:*
• Cut the goat's milk cheese into thin slices. Stir together the spices and tomato purée. Slice the fresh tomatoes.
• Put a slice of the cheese in each aubergine pocket. Fill up with tomato mixture.
• Put the slices in a well-oiled ovenproof dish. Finally place a slice of tomato on top.
• Heat the "pizzaiola" at 180—200° for about 5 minutes. Serve immediately.

## Mixed salad with dandelion leaves

*Fresh, tender dandelion leaves mixed with some other kind of lettuce, such as lollorosso, for the colour. This salad is topped with yellow dandelion flowers and a well-rounded vinaigrette. I usually make a lot of vinaigrette that I then keep in a bottle in the fridge.*

Tender dandelion leaves
Equal amount of lollorosso (or other sort)
Dandelion flowers

*Vinaigrette:*
1/2 dl balsamic vinegar
1 1/2–2 dl extra virgin olive oil
1 tbsp Dijon mustard
1/2–1 tsp herbal salt
2 tsp dried tarragon
2 tsp dried marjoram
2 tsp dried thyme
3 cloves garlic if desired

• Rinse the dandelion and lettuce leaves and leave to drain well. Divide the leaves into smaller pieces and mix together in a bowl.

*Vinaigrette:*
• Blend all the ingredients in a mixer, or whisk them very vigorously into a fairly thick vinaigrette.
• Pour over the desired amount of vinaigrette and decorate with dandelion flowers. Serve as a side dish with meat, fish or pasta.

## Ruccola salad with Parmesan cheese

*Generous slices of Parmesan cheese spread over freshly picked ruccola lettuce. Our own ruccola lettuce is special. I bought the seeds myself in a little shop in Venice and carried them all the way home to Rosendal. This tremendously good dish can be enjoyed with some sun-dried tomatoes and balsam dressing at our café.*

Ruccola lettuce (2 pots)
200 g Parmesan cheese
15–20 sun-dried tomatoes

• Rinse and divide the lettuce and arrange on four decorative plates. Cut large slices of Parmesan cheese, using a cheese slicer. Put the slices on the lettuce and spread over some sun-dried tomatoes.
• Sprinkle with balsam vinaigrette (see Caprese) and serve with bread.

## Caprese
## (salad with tomato and mozzarella)
*(4 servings)*

*A meal that I ate almost every day when I lived in Italy. I am really pleased that caprese has been so much in demand at the café. Sometimes when we have lots of tomatoes we put a whole sprig of tomatoes on the plate!*

4 sweet, ripe tomatoes
350–400 g mozzarella
3–4 sprigs fresh basil

*Vinaigrette:*
Salt
Pepper
1 dl extra virgin olive oil
1/3 dl balsamic vinegar

A variation of spiced butter to have with grilled meat. Mix the butter with nasturtium flowers and chive flowers. Add herbal salt, finely chopped chives and basil. Form into the desired shape and keep the butter cold until serving. *Previous page*: zucchini flowers. *Opposite page*: caprese.

- Slice the tomatoes and arrange on a decorative serving dish. Sandwich with slices of mozzarella.
- Stir together salt, pepper, olive oil and balsamic vinegar. Pour the dressing over the salad and spread the basil leaves on top. Serve with bread.

## Feta salad

*(4 servings)*

*Feta salad is served every day at the garden café during the summer and early autumn. It is most popular, of course, when we can serve our own tomatoes with it. It is fantastic firstly to see the tomatoes hanging on their branches in the glasshouse, and then to taste this sweet, sun-ripened jewel.*

1 head of lettuce
1/2 cucumber
2 large onions
4 thick slices of feta (125 g each)
2 dl black olives
15–20 basil leaves

*Vinaigrette:*
1/2 dl white wine vinegar
1 1/2–2 dl extra virgin olive oil
1 tbsp dried basil
Salt and freshly ground black pepper

- Rinse and shred the lettuce. Peel the cucumber with a cheese slice and cut into pieces. Mix.
- Cut the onions into rings and the feta cheese into cubes.
- Place the salad on a plate. Arrange the feta cheese, onion rings, olives and basil leaves on top.

*Vinaigrette:*
- Vigorously whisk together all the ingredients. Add salt and pepper to taste. Pour the dressing over the salad and serve it with bread and a glass of beer.

## Curry-pickled herring

*(4 servings)*

*We serve curry-pickled herring at the garden café at Easter and in the early summer, before Midsummer, when every Swede longs for pickled herring! I make it with matjes herring, but you can make it with freshened salt-pickled fillets.*

4 fillets of matjes herring
1–2 red apples
1 red onion
About 30 g butter
1/2–1 tbsp curry
1 dl mayonnaise
1/2–1 dl crème fraiche
1 sprig dill

- Cut the herring fillets into 1 cm wide pieces. Core and chop the apple. Finely chop the onion.
- Fry the butter and the curry in a saucepan.
- Mix everything into the mayonnaise and add enough crème fraiche. Using scissors, snip the dill over the top. Serve by itself with potatoes and boiled eggs, or as a spread on top of a slice of dark bread.

## Stock-boiled fillet of beef with basil sauce

*A heavenly dish! Serve the fillet of beef cold, cut into thin slices and accompanied by a fragrant, dark green basil sauce.*

About 1/2 kg fillet of beef
3–4 stock cubes (ox stock)
A few bay leaves
2–3 cloves garlic

*Basil sauce:*
2 cloves garlic
3–4 tbsp balsamic vinegar
About 100 g basil leaves
About 1/2 dl extra virgin olive oil
1/2 dl stock from the fillet of beef
Salt and pepper

- Trim and truss the meat, so that it keeps its shape.
- Boil up the stock with the bay leaves and garlic. Put in the beef and simmer gently for 12–15 minutes. It should be pink inside. Take out the meat and leave to cool.

*Sauce:*
- Blend the garlic, balsamic vinegar, basil leaves and olive oil in a mixer. Then add the stock. Use more olive oil if necessary. Salt and pepper to taste.

*To serve:*
Thinly slice the fillet of beef and arrange on a plate. Pour over some of the sauce and serve the rest of it in a bowl, it'll get eaten! Serve with roasted potatoes with sesame seeds.

*Opposite page:* poppy baguette, feta cheese salad, spring pasta and penne with pesto.
*Following spread:* frittata, open sandwich wth egg and roe.
*Page 150:* A. Stock-boiled fillet of beef with basil sauce. B . Saffron pasta. C. Sweet-and-sour cherry tomatoes. D. Oven roasted potato wedges with sesame seeds.
*Page 153:* A. Smoked herring with chive sauce and French potato salad. B. Curry-pickled herring with jacket potatoes.

## Feta cheese, tomato and black olive flan
*(5–6 servings)*
*A wonderful summer flan. Serve with a crisp green salad and a glass of beer!*

3–4 frozen sheets of puff pastry

*Filling:*
30 g butter
100 g feta cheese
1/2 dl double cream
5 tbsp fresh basil, chopped
5 tomatoes
Black olives

• Defrost the sheets of puff pastry and put them in a flan ring. Prick the bottom with a fork.
• Melt the butter and add the cream and feta cheese, chopped in smallish pieces. Let it all melt together into a thick and smooth mixture. Add the freshly chopped basil.
• Divide the tomatoes into halves. Place them on the pastry and cover with the cheese mixture. Sprinkle with black olives.
• Bake the flan at 225° for about 20 minutes. Decorate with basil leaves.

## Frittata
*(4 servings)*

*I often ate frittata in Italy. It's a kind of omelette. You can flavour the frittata with whatever you have to hand. My favourite is this one, with fresh herbs and Parmesan cheese. Can be served hot or cold. It goes well with a ruccola and tomato salad.*

1 red onion, chopped fine
8 eggs
100 g freshly grated Parmesan cheese
3 tbsp fresh basil, chopped
3 tbsp fresh parsley, chopped
3 tbsp fresh chives, chopped
Butter for frying
Salt and pepper to taste

• Melt the butter and fry the finely chopped onion until soft.
• Grate the Parmesan cheese and whisk the eggs. Finely chop the fresh herbs. Mix all the ingredients and fry the frittata in butter like an ordinary omelette. Cut up into appetising pieces before serving.

## Sauces
*(4–5 servings)*

*It is very easy to make your own sauces to have with smoked fish and pâté, for example. These recipes can serve as suggestions:*

*Roe sauce for smoked salmon:*
5 dl crème fraiche
1/2 dl kefir
2 dl whitefish roe
1 tbsp fresh lemon balm, chopped fine
1/2 tbsp lemon juice
2 tbsp fresh dill, chopped fine

• Mix together all the ingredients and leave the sauce to chill for an hour or so before serving.

*Chive sauce for smoked Baltic herring:*
4 dl crème fraiche
1 dl sour cream
5 tbsp chives, chopped fine
1/2 tbsp herbal salt

• Mix all the ingredients and leave the sauce to chill an hour or so before serving.

*Herb garden sauce for fish or shellfish pâtés:*
4 dl crème fraiche
1 dl kefir
2 tbsp dried basil
2 tbsp dried chervil
2 tbsp dried thyme
2 tbsp fresh parsley, chopped fine
2 tbsp fresh dill, chopped fine
1/2 tbsp herbal salt

• Mix all the ingredients and leave the sauce to chill for an hour or so before serving.

## Oven-roasted potato wedges with sesame seeds
*Crispy potato wedges for serving with meat. A good side dish for a buffet.*

1 1/2 kg potatoes
1/2–1 dl olive oil
1/2 dl sesame seeds
2 tbsp fresh thyme, chopped
2 cloves garlic

*For decoration:*
A few sprigs fresh thyme

• Peel the potatoes and divide into wedges. Brush with the olive oil and roll them in the sesame seeds.
• Cover the bottom of an ovenproof dish with olive oil. Spread out the potato wedges. Sprinkle with pressed garlic and thyme.
• Bake the wedges at 200–225° for about 20–25 minutes. Decorate with fresh thyme when serving.

## French potato salad
*French, because it is flavoured with Dijon mustard. Capers give it a salty tang and red peppers a decorative colour. This potato salad is just as good cold as hot. Serve with gammon, smoked ham or smoked fish.*

About 800–1000 g firm potatoes or new potatoes
1 large red pepper
1 leek
About 1 1/2 dl extra virgin olive oil
2–3 tbsp balsamic vinegar
3–4 tbsp Dijon mustard
2 tbsp thyme
Salt
Freshly ground black pepper
5 tbsp capers
1 bunch fresh chives

• Peel the potatoes and divide into smallish pieces. Boil in lightly salted water until soft but still fairly firm.
• Chop the pepper into small pieces. Cut the leek into thin strips.
• Using a mixer, blend the olive oil, balsamic vinegar, mustard into a rich dressing. Add salt and pepper to taste.
• Put the hot potatoes on a serving dish and pour over the dressing. Mix well and sprinkle with capers and finely chopped chives.

## Basil potatoes
*(4–5 servings)*

*Different kinds of potato salad are a popular side dish to the café's meat and fish dishes. This is practical because they can be served hot, warm or cold. The potato salads are adapted to the season.*

About 800–1000 g new potatoes
3–4 dl fresh basil leaves
1/2 dl parsley, coarsely chopped
1 1/2 dl extra virgin olive oil
4 tbsp white wine vinegar
1 dl Parmesan cheese, finely grated
1–2 cloves of garlic
Salt
Pepper

VARM POTATIS
MED SMOR
SICKI SALAD
1 M. M r

PURIELOR

VINIGRETT
MAI

'94

• Brush and clean the potatoes and divide into smaller pieces if they are large.
• Boil up lightly salted water and cook the potatoes for about 15 minutes until soft.
• Chop the basil, parsley leaves and garlic together, using a food processor if you like. Add vinegar and oil, a few drops at a time, mixing continuously.
• Add the grated parmesan cheese and mix well. Flavour with salt and pepper.
• Pour the sauce over the hot potatoes and mix. Decorate with some basil leaves. These potatoes go well with smoked salmon or smoked ham.

## Spring pasta
(About 4 servings)

*A very practical dish since it is just as good hot or cold, with or without accessories. Use the spring vegetables that are available, for example carrots, broccoli and spring onions.*

500 g mixed spring vegetables
1 stock cube
50–100 g butter
500 g pasta, penne or twists
Water
Olive oil
Salt

*Sauce:*
1 dl red wine vinegar
3–4 dl extra virgin olive oil
4–5 cloves garlic
2 tbsp dried basil
1/2 tbsp herbal salt
Pinch freshly ground black pepper

• Rinse and clean the vegetables. Cut large vegetables into smaller pieces.
• Boil up the stock and add vegetables according to boiling time. Pour off the stock. Stir some butter into the vegetables.
• Boil the pasta in water with a little olive oil and salt. Pour off the water. Mix the pasta with the vegetables and pour over the sauce. Serve with slices of tomato and basil leaves, and perhaps two slices of smoked ham and a piece of bread.

*Sauce:*
• Using a mixer, blend all the ingredients into a light sauce (or whisk them very vigorously by hand, in which case crush the garlic). This sauce will keep for a couple of weeks in the fridge.

## Saffron pasta
(About 4 servings)

*At Easter we serve golden yellow pasta in the café. Coloured eggs, black olives and smoked ham are tasty accessories.*

500 g pasta, penne or twists
3–4 cloves garlic
1–2 g saffron
1 dl extra virgin olive oil
2 tbsp orange vinegar (or white wine vinegar)
1/2 tbsp dried basil
Salt and freshly ground black pepper

*For serving:*
Freshly grated Parmesan cheese
2–3 tbsp fresh basil, chopped

• Boil the pasta in the water with salt and a few tablespoons of olive oil.
• Finely chop the cloves of garlic and crush them in a mortar together with the saffron.
• Fry the oil, garlic and saffron in a pot. Add the vinegar, basil, salt and pepper. Pour the yellow sauce over the pasta and stir. Sprinkle with grated Parmesan and freshly chopped basil.

## Potato and leek soup
(About 4 servings)

*Smooth, creamy and tasty…*

1/2 kg potatoes
2 large leeks
2–3 tbsp butter
6 dl good vegetable stock
About 2 dl double cream
Salt
Freshly ground black pepper
5 tbsp fresh chervil and chives, chopped fine.

• Rinse the leek and cut into thin strips. Peel the potatoes and divide into smaller pieces.
• Fry the butter and leek in a saucepan. Put in the pieces of potato and add the stock. Boil until the potatoes and the leek are meltingly soft, about 25–30 minutes.
• Blend the soup in a food processor or strain it through a wire sieve. Stir in the cream and let the soup simmer on a low heat until warm. Add salt and pepper to taste. Sprinkle with the freshly chopped herbs. Serve the soup with bread.

Stock-boiled spring vegetables in a simple sauce of melted butter, herbal salt and blue poppyseeds. A delicacy!

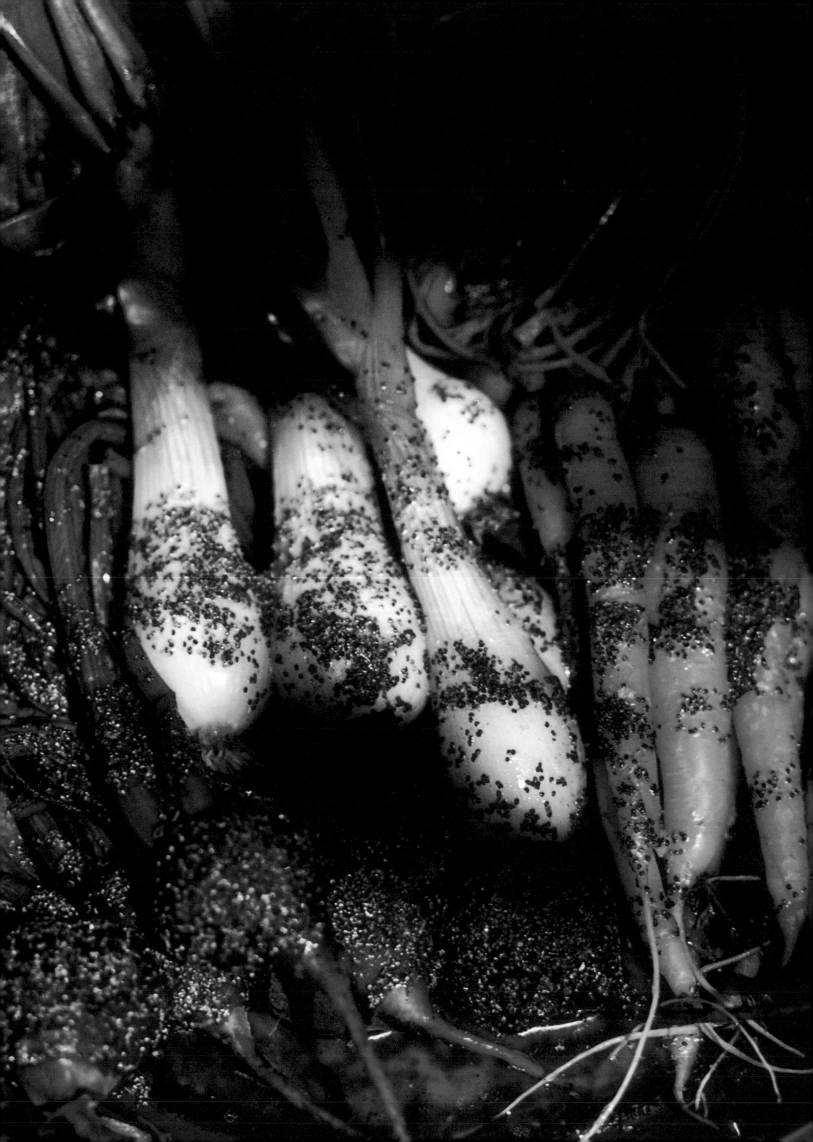

## Nettle soup

*(About 4 servings)*

*A very simple but much appreciated soup, made from the very first spring vegetables. Knee-high boots and rubber gloves are necessary equipment!*

2 l tender nettle leaves
1 piece of leek
Water
Salt
3 tbsp butter
1 tbsp flour
1 1/2 l good stock
2 tsp fennel and aniseed mixed
Salt and pepper
About 1 dl double cream

*For serving:*
Egg halves
Fresh chives, chopped fine

• Rinse the nettles well in cold water and squeeze them dry. Finely slice the leek and put it with the nettles into lightly salted boiling water. Boil for about 12 minutes. Pour off the water. Mince the nettles in a mixer.
• Fry butter and flour in a saucepan. Dilute with the stock. Tie the aniseed and fennel in a piece of cloth and put the packet into the stock. Allow to boil together for 7–8 minutes. Add the nettles. Flavour with salt, pepper and cream. Boil for a further 3–4 minutes. Serve the soup with egg halves and finely chopped chives.

## Currant preserve

*A wonderful condiment to have with many meat dishes, with or instead of jelly.*

1 l red currants

*Solution:*
1 dl water
2 dl sugar
1/2 dl vinegar essence
1 whole cinnamon stick
4–5 cloves
4–5 allspice peppercorns

• Pick over and clean the currants. Measure up one litre. Mix all the ingredients to the solution in a saucepan. Bring to the boil. Boil for a few minutes.
• Add the red currants and simmer for about 10 minutes under a lid. Carefully stir the currants now and then.
• Pour the red currants into hot, well-cleaned jars. Seal immediately. Store in a cool place and leave for at least one week before enjoying them with, for example, roast lamb or spring chicken.

## Bottled crystalized ginger with lemon grass

*Fresh ginger, or preserved as here, is very good in stir-fried food. Crystalized ginger can be eaten with both ice-cream and grilled cutlets.*

500 g fresh ginger
Scant 14 dl sugar
1 1/2   l water
4 tbsp lemon grass

• Peel the ginger and divide into pieces, 2–3 cm long. Boil in water for about 40 minutes until soft.
• Boil up the sugar and water. Put in the ginger and allow to simmer for about 30 minutes. Add lemon grass and simmer for a few minutes more.
• Transfer the ginger to hot, well-cleaned jars. Pour over the hot liquid and seal in the usual way.

Marinated olives.

# SOLTORKADE TOMATER

FÖRST HITTA INTET

UR INTET GÖRA ALLT

UR ALLT FORMA ENERGI

UR ENERGI SKAPA EN VÄRLD

PÅ DENNA VÄRLD PLACERA EN

## TOMAT

FEMTON MILJARDER ÅR
AV FÖRBEREDELSE

CIRKA TIO MINUTER FRÅN STAN

...OM MAN GÅR

## Spicy apple chutney

*Chutney is a good condiment for all sorts of grilled meat. This is a hot chutney that is easy to make.*

1 kg firm cooking apples
1 large onion
2–3 tbsp freshly grated ginger
2 dl apple cider vinegar
6 dl sugar
3 dl raisins
1 tsp salt
3–4 tsp curry
4 large cloves garlic, crushed

• Peel, core and coarsely chop the apples. Finely chop the onion. Grate the ginger.
• Put all the ingredients into a saucepan and bring to the boil. Simmer the mixture for about one hour.
• Pour the chutney into hot, well-cleaned jars and seal immediately. Leave to mature for two or three weeks before serving.

## Marinated garlic

*Always appreciated. Keeps for several months.*

About 50 cloves garlic, fairly large
1–1 1/2 dl balsamic vinegar
1 1/2 tsp thyme
1 1/2 tsp tarragon
1 1/2 tsp chervil
2 small peppers
About 1 1/2 dl extra virgin olive oil

• Boil the garlic cloves in water for one minute. Rinse the cloves with cold water and peel them.
• Put the garlic cloves into a glass jar with a lid and pour over the vinegar until it covers them. Put the lid on and leave for two days.
• Pour off the vinegar.
• Mix the spices with the olive oil. Alternate the cloves and the spiced oil (keeping the spices) in a glass jar and leave for at least one week before savouring.

## Marinated olives

*Black and green olives mixed and marinated in extra virgin olive oil, garlic and spices. It's very easy to make yourself and is a much appreciated present. Olives are also nice to serve with drinks, for example.*

Black and green olives with pits
Bay leaves
Garlic, partly for crushing, partly whole cloves
Dried thyme
Dried tarragon
Dried chervil
Herbal salt
Extra virgin olive oil

• Put the olives into a bowl. Press some cloves of garlic over the olives and add some whole cloves. Spice to taste. Pour over some extra virgin olive oil and stir. Leave the olives in a cool place for a few days before they are savoured. You can keep them in the fridge for weeks without having to put them in jars.

## "Sun-dried" tomatoes

*A real delicacy which can be made at home in your own oven.*

For 100 g dried tomatoes or 1 jar preserved in oil (200 ml) you need:

8–10 tomatoes
4 cloves garlic
2 tbsp tarragon, parsley, basil or other good spice
1 tbsp herbal salt
1 1/2 dl olive oil, extra virgin

• Divide the tomatoes into 4 segments. Place them on a baking sheet and put them in a 60° oven for about 6–8 hours. Turn the tomato segments occasionally and make sure they don't get burnt towards the end of the time.
• Peel the garlic cloves.
• Salt the tomatoes and put them with the garlic and the spices in a well-cleaned glass jar with a screw top. Carefully pour over the oil. This is excellent to use with pasta sauces, flans, salads or why not in your home-baked bread. The tomatoes will keep for several months in the jar if the oil is of good quality and covers the tomatoes and spices properly.

## Sweet-and-sour cherry tomatoes

*These small, delicate yellow and red cherry tomatoes will light up the buffet table or will be a joy to behold in a glass jar when waiting to be used.*

1/2 kg yellow cherry tomatoes
1/2 kg red cherry tomatoes

*Solution:*
5 dl white wine vinegar
9 dl sugar
4 whole cinnamon sticks
7 cloves
5 allspice peppercorns
1 1/2 tsp herbal salt

• Rinse and tail the tomatoes.

*Solution:*
• Boil up the vinegar, sugar and spices. Allow to simmer for about 10 minutes.
• Put the tomatoes on a colourful dish and pour over the hot solution. Stir the tomatoes around. Leave to stand for two hours before serving. (*Continued on page* 169.)

*Tomatoes are crushed*
*at the beginning of July*
*for use in cooking.*

Tomater krossas
i början av juli —
används i matlagningen

Tapenade. Ingredients for spicy apple chutney. *Opposite page:* marinated peppers.
*Following spread:* Parmesan cheese, sesame baguette, spiced vinegar, spiced olive oil, red "pesto" and pesto.

## COTTAGE CHEESE BALLS WITH HERBS

*I use cottage cheese from Borgvattnet's dairy. I sometimes serve these little balls at a buffet. Sometimes I marinate them in extra virgin olive oil and herbs, then bottle them with incredibly beautiful results!*

150 g cottage cheese
1 tsp herbal salt
Alternative I chives, finely chopped
Alternative II fresh thyme, finely chopped

*For marinating:*
Dried herbs, for example: oregano, marjoram, thyme
Extra virgin olive oil

• Mix the herbal salt into the cheese. Make small balls, about 10. Roll the balls in chives or thyme.

*Marinating:*
• Place the balls in a glass jar. Alternate with extra herbs and cover the balls with olive oil. Seal and store in a cool place.

• If you are going to use the tomatoes on a later occasion, you can put them into hot, well-cleaned jars. Strain the solution and pour over the tomatoes. Put some spices in each jar and seal in the usual way.

## Marinated peppers

*Peppers have wonderful colours to relish with meat or on the buffet table. You can also save it for winter salads or serve it as an appetizer, with newly toasted bread.*

About 1 kg mixed yellow, green and red peppers

*For marinating:*
Extra virgin olive oil
1 red onion, chopped fine
6 cloves garlic, chopped fine
Salt and freshly ground black pepper
4 dl white wine vinegar
3 dl water
4 bay leaves
4 sprigs fresh thyme
7–8 coriander seeds
4–5 peppercorns

*For preserving:*
About 1 l extra virgin olive oil
Extra bay leaves
Extra thyme
Extra garlic cloves
3–4 sprigs fresh basil

• Peel and slice the peppers lengthways. Make sure to remove all the white pith and the small seeds.
• Fry the onion and garlic in extra virgin olive oil. Salt and pepper. Add vinegar, water and spices. Boil everything together for a few minutes. Pour the marinade over the slices of pepper and leave to stand cold for about 10 hours.
• Remove the pepper slices and put them in well-cleaned jars together with the bay leaves, thyme, garlic and basil. Cover with olive oil and seal. The peppers will keep for several months. If you are going to use directly after marinating I always mix one part marinade with two parts extra virgin olive oil. You can serve the pepper and olive oil marinade in a beautiful dish sprinkled with fresh herbs and cloves of garlic. Enjoy!

## Marinated goat cheese

*We use goat cheese from Borgvattnet's dairy. It is marinated in extra virgin olive oil and herbs. There are many variations and here are a few examples:*

Goat's milk cheese
Bay leaves
Dried thyme
Dried basil
Dried chervil
Garlic, according to taste
Extra virgin olive oil

• Cut the cheese into small pieces. Put the pieces in a beautiful jar with a screw-top, being careful not to get the edge messy. Alternate with the herbs and garlic, if liked. Finally pour over the olive oil and seal. Let the cheese stand for a week or two before eating.

## Tapenade

*Tapenade is an olive paste from Provence that is the perfect topping for small pieces of toast served with drinks. It is grey and drab in colour, almost grotesque, but its taste is divine.*

1 1/2 dl black olives, pitted
7—8 anchovies
2 tbsp capers
2 cloves of garlic
Juice of 1/2 a lemon

Spiced olive oil. *Opposite page:* spiced vinegar.

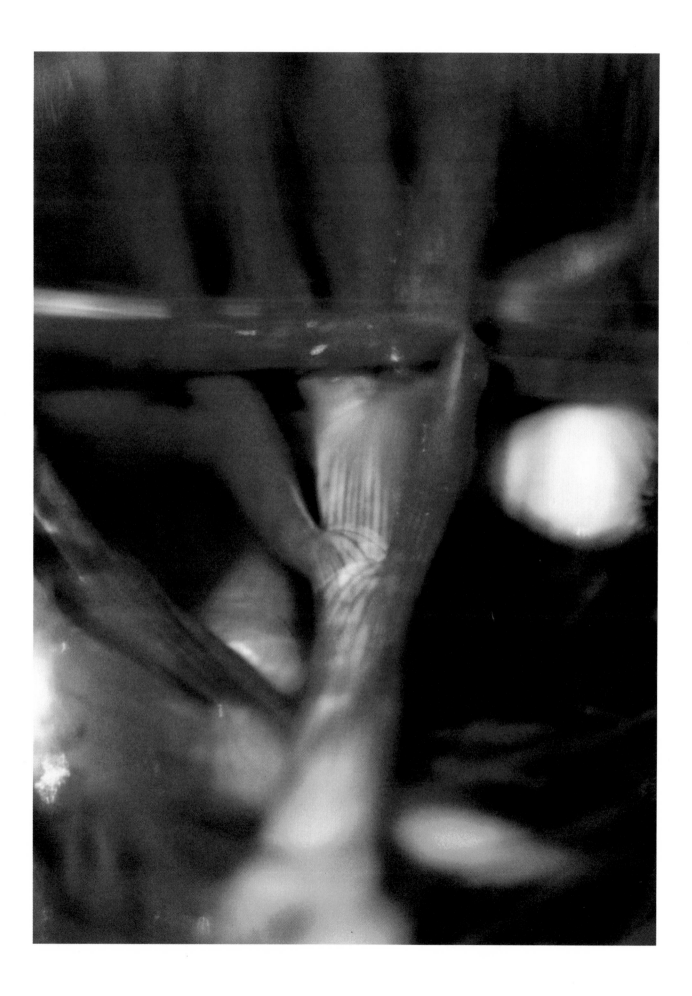

5 tbsp fresh basil, chopped
Freshly ground black pepper
1/2–1 dl extra virgin olive oil

• Blend all the ingredients into a smooth mass in a mixer. Adding oil, bring to a suitable consistency. You can make tapenade in larger amounts and fill jars, sealing in the usual way.

## Pesto

*(Makes about 2 1/2 dl)*

*The name basil comes from the Greek word basileus, which means king. For me, too, this wonderful plant is the king of herbs. When the gardeners have watered the basil in the glasshouse next to the café, its fragrance spreads all the way into our kitchen. Pesto, a sauce made of basil that is served with freshly cooked pasta, is a famous, classic dish from Northern Italy. The "real" way to make it is by crushing the leaves into a sauce in a mortar, but you can do it just as well in a mixer.*

6 dl fresh basil leaves
4 cloves garlic
Some coarse salt
1/2 –1 dl pine kernels
1–1 1/2 dl extra virgin olive oil
1–1 1/2 dl fresh Parmesan cheese, grated

*In the mortar:*
• Put the basil, pine kernels, garlic and some coarse salt in the mortar. Pound and mix into a smooth mass. Add the grated Parmesan cheese and enough olive oil to make a suitable consistency.

*In the mixer:*
• Blend everything except the Parmesan into a smooth mass. Add the oil drop by drop. Lower the speed and blend in the freshly grated Parmesan cheese.

## Red "pesto"

*(Makes about 2 1/2 dl)*

*This is a variation of pesto made with tomatoes and which is amazingly good! We call it red pesto.*

4 large ripe, sweet tomatoes. (Can be replaced by about 1 dl good tomato purée.)
2–3 cloves garlic
1/2 dl pine kernels
About 1 1/2 dl fresh basil leaves
1/2–1 dl extra virgin olive oil
Salt and newly ground pepper
1/2 dl Parmesan cheese, newly grated

• Peel the tomatoes. Divide them and remove the centres.
• Using a mixer, blend the flesh of the tomatoes or tomato purée with the garlic, pine kernels, basil, half the olive oil, salt and pepper. Add more olive oil to bring to the required consistency. Mix in the Parmesan. Serve red pesto as a sauce with pasta or lightly cooked spring vegetables with some tasty bread.

## Spiced oils

*Your own spiced oils are easy to make and fun to use. It is also easy to add your very own favourite flavour to the oil. As always, choose an olive oil of the very highest quality and fresh or dried herbs and spices according to your own taste. Remember that if you are using fresh spices, rinse them only if absolutely necessary, drying them thoroughly afterwards.*

Extra virgin olive oil
Herbs, spices
Beautiful bottles

• Poke the herbs and spices into the bottle. Pour in the olive oil and seal. Make sure that the herbs and spices are covered by the oil, or else they might go mouldy. Let the oil absorb the flavouring for at least a week before using.

Beautiful and tasty combinations:

Fresh garlic, basil
Fresh garlic and a sprig of thyme
Sprigs of thyme and tarragon
Sprigs of rosemary
Red and green Spanish peppers

## Spiced vinegar

*Spiced vinegar has long been used in Southern Europe. Raspberry vinegar is excellent to use for heightening the flavour of a good sauce. Ginger vinegar gives stir-fried vegetables an extra kick and a basil-flavoured vinegar adds a masterful touch to the simplest tomato salad. It is also pleasant to have your own vinegar on the kitchen shelf. White wine vinegar or apple cider vinegar is the most beautiful, of course, but a red wine vinegar with whole ginger or cloves of garlic, maybe both, is worth trying.*

• Put the berries or spices in a glass jar or a wide-necked bottle. Pour over the vinegar and seal. Leave the vinegar to mature in a light place for about 2–3 weeks.
• Strain off the berries or spices. Pour the fragrant and beautifully coloured vinegar into a glass bottle and seal.

Till Monika
från Peter

Du visar
det sköna
och gör
det goda!

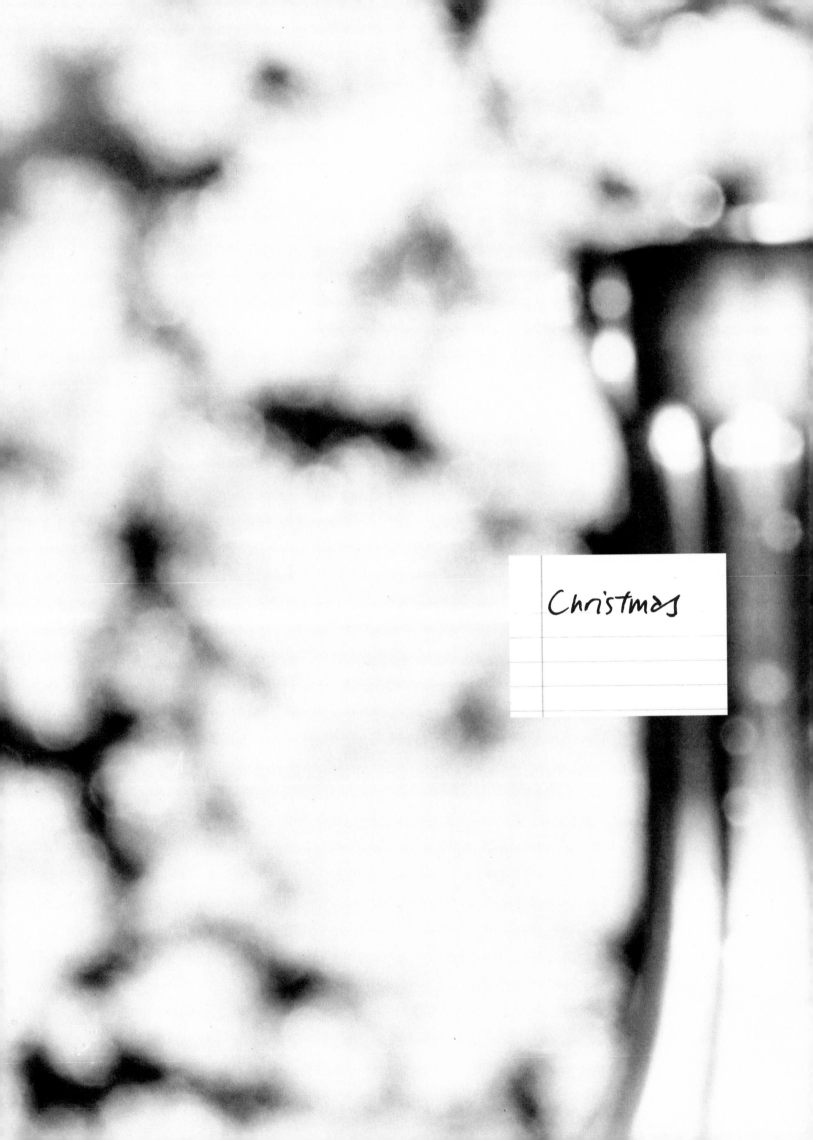

Christmas

# The Christmas Fair

We sometimes leave Rosendal's garden in the late autumn to go for a trip abroad. These journeys have taken us to Italy (Tuscany, Umbria, Lombardy), France (Provence and Bourgogne) and Spain (Catalonia and Andalusia).

We have contemplated the most beautiful gardens of Europe, in the company of artists such as Picasso, Matisse, da Vinci, Giacometti and Goya. We have been on a wine tasting course at a vineyard, seen flamenco and of course eaten some of the specialities of each region.

Every new encounter, of course, gives us inspiration for our imminent Christmas Fair: Can we do this? Just think if we… Maybe we can… Look, such colours… Smell those scents… Yes, there are lots of ideas to set our imagination working.

Charlott Winqvist, who works in our garden shop, and I also have a fondness for early mornings at the market squares or market halls of each new small town. We have taken so many different bags of spices, conserves, different types of flour or sugar, chocolate sweets, pasta variations and so on home with us in our specially bought suitcase, with the express purpose of putting them on the shelves at the Christmas Fair, or for using in our own experiments to find new favourites for our customers. So, just think, the next time someone takes a jar or a paper bag down from the shelf it might just well originate from Grasse, Sienna or Granada.

When we arrive back at the beginning of November we are all filled with a special feeling. Our emotions fluctuate between joy, expectancy and exhaustion. For it is now that we need all the strength and imagination we can muster. New and old ideas must be bandied back and forth. This is the time when we also have to have a completely different assortment to sell, everything from toys to kitchen utensils to furniture.

There is intense activity on every hand. To start with we have to package our own dried herbs from the summer. They are arranged in little bouquets of tasteful herb mixtures, or are used in our own herbal tea. They are packed partly in bags and partly in somewhat larger cartons. We do everything by hand, of course, and with the utmost care. Finally, as a crowning glory, we add a characteristic label, often hand-written.

An endless variety of transparent vinegar and olive oil bottles are filled with good, sensuous and beautiful combinations of herbs. Thousands of litres of vinegar that have stood maturing in the café windows during the autumn are strained and poured into smaller, darker bottles.

Jams and marmalades are made with every possible fruit available and flavoured with some special Christmas spice, such as ginger, cinnamon or aniseed.

Gradually more and more imaginative preserves are created. Each more colourful than the other. One idea often breeds another. Some are favourites that recur every year, often accompanied by a specific ceremony when they are made. As when Malin Löfstrand, who usually works as master gardener, and I team up. We work late into the night or early morning. The first budding Christmas feelings are awoken when we taste the first glögg (mulled wine). We both know which duty we each have. I make the sugar-liquid, boil the pears, take them out of the cooking pot and place them gracefully in the hot jars. Then I send them over to Malin, who is phenomenal at pouring in the hot sugar-liquid, getting the rubber rings in place and sealing the jars. We have, of course, peeled each pear, striving to keep the stalk left on, which it doesn't always agree to… We use up about 200 kg pears during the whole Christmas Fair. Proud, yellow almost orange saffron pears, deep-red lingonberry pears spiced with cinnamon and cloves, and yellowish-white vanilla pears with a thick, generous vanilla pod in each jar adorn the shelves for a few hours every day during the Christmas Fair.

Together with a few persevering colleagues in the bakery, I bake more or less round the clock. Gingersnaps, saffron rusks, ginger cakes, klenäter, Lucia buns, Stollen cake and Panettone are just a few of our rich assortment.

Spices are crushed and ground. Doughs are kneaded and shaped. Chocolate is melted and rusks are dried. There is feverish activity that spreads its tantalising smells and scents far beyond our own garden. Certain choice cakes or pastries are wrapped in sumptuous cellophane with broad, red ribbons. Biscuits and small cakes find their way into paper bags or cartons.

Like happy little children, initially at least, we shape gingersnap dough into long loaves and wrap them in cellophane, together with the recipe. And thus, we have one of the most sought after products of the Fair. Seventy-five kilos of dough a day is not unusual. Just think, the weight of a whole human being!

At the same time we serve fifty different cakes, pastries and buns in the garden café. The usual selection, enlarged with tempting Christmas specialities. This gives our guests a hard time choosing. Usually they end up with their favourite cake and a Christmas cake, after perhaps having eaten a Christmas sandwich, a Christmas buffet or a bowl of hot, golden-yellow saffron pudding. Most people stay for a long time, imbibing the tastes and smells and inspecting their newly purchased additions to the kitchen shelf.

When dusk approaches, they leave for home with a carefully chosen Christmas tree, a pot of decorated Christmas flowers or a simple hyacinth under their arm.

A glass of home-made glögg served outside the café, to the accompaniment of crackling wood fires, serves to keep most people warm all the way home.

## Per's glögg

1 tbsp whole cardamoms, ½ tbsp whole cloves, 1 cinnamon stick, 1 piece of ginger, 3 ½ dl water, 5 dl undiluted blackcurrant juice, vodka to taste.

Crush the cardamoms and cloves in a mortar. Boil the water with all the spices under a lid for 10 minutes. Pour in the juice and bring back to the boil. Leave to draw for a couple of hours. Sieve off the spices. Heat and lace the glögg with vodka if you want. Serve with raisins and almonds.

## Ginger nuts

*(Makes about 35)*

125 g butter
1 dl sugar
1 tsp golden syrup
1/2 egg
1/2 tsp ginger
1/2 tsp cinnamon
1/2–1 tsp freshly crushed cardamom
About 3 1/2 dl flour
1 tsp bicarbonate

*For garnishing:*
About 35 blanched almonds

• Stir together the butter, sugar and syrup.
• Add the egg and spices.
• Mix the bicarbonate into the flour. Stir it into the mixture and work together thoroughly.
• Shape into round balls, about 35, and put them on a greased baking sheet. Press an almond into each ball and flatten them a little.
• Bake at 175° for about 15–18 minutes.

## Rosendal's spicy gingersnaps

*(Makes about 350 small or 175 larger biscuits)*

*This dough keeps very well, so you don't need to bake it all at once. Just make sure not to store it too cold or else it goes dry and crumbly. These gingersnaps are crunchy and somewhat hard.*

4 1/2 dl golden syrup
300 g butter (soft, room temperature)
4 1/2 dl sugar
1 egg
4 tsp freshly ground cloves
6 tsp ground cinnamon
4 tsp ground ginger
4 tsp freshly crushed cardamoms
13–15 dl flour

• Boil up the syrup. Stir. Leave to cool.
• Stir in the sugar, eggs, spices and the butter (at room temperature).
• Add the flour, the smaller amount (save the rest for the baking). Work together thoroughly so that the ingredients are properly mixed. Leave in a cool, but not cold, place until the next day.
• Roll out the dough very thinly and cut out Christmas shapes (such as gingerbread men, houses, animals) using cookie cutters. Place them on greased baking sheets.
• Bake at 180–200° for about 8 minutes.

## Saffron rusks

*(Makes about 45–50)*

120 g almonds
2 packets (1 g) saffron + 1 sugar lump
2 eggs
2 dl sugar
1 tsp salt
5–6 dl flour
1 tsp baking powder
100 g dark, Belgian cooking chocolate, chopped coarsely

*For glazing:*
1 egg white

• Finely grind one third of the almonds and chop the rest *very* coarsely. Crush the saffron together with the sugar lump.
• Mix the almond, egg, sugar, saffron and salt. Add 3 dl of the flour mixed with the bicarbonate. Then add the lightly floured chocolate. Finally mix in the rest of the flour, a little at a time. Make sure not to use too much flour.
• Roll out into lengths and place them on greased baking sheets. Brush with the egg white.
• Bake the lengths at 180° for about 15–20 minutes.
• Cut them into rusks and dry them at 100° for about 30–40 minutes.

## Klenäter

*(Makes about 35–40)*

*No Christmas without klenäter, that's what I've always thought ever since I ate my first one as a child. Klenäter are traditional Swedish twist cookies, deep-fried in oil.*

50 g butter
1 egg
1 egg yolk
1/2 dl icing sugar
1 tbsp snaps or cognac
Grated peel of 1/2 lemon
2 1/2 dl flour

*For deep-frying:*
300–500 g coconut fat

*For garnishing:*
Sugar mixed with cinnamon

• Melt the butter and leave to cool.
• Vigorously stir the egg, egg yolk, and icing sugar.
• Add the cognac, lemon peel, butter and flour.
• Cover the dough with cling film and leave over night in a cold place.
• Roll out the dough very thinly. Using a pastry wheel, cut into pieces of about 10–12 cm long and 3 cm wide. Make a slit in the middle of each piece. Thread a corner through the slit to twist the cookie.

• Melt the coconut fat and heat it through. Do a test to see if it is hot enough: fry a little piece of dough. If it quickly turns golden brown, then the temperature is right.
• Taking a few cookies at a time, fry on both sides. Leave to drain on kitchen paper and then dip them in the mixture of cinnamon and sugar.

## Nut meringue sandwich with cream
*(Makes about 15)*

*Sometimes we have lots of egg whites left over. It was on such an occasion that this meringue "sandwich" came about.*

4 egg whites
2 dl icing sugar
1 1/2–2 dl hazelnuts, chopped fine
Whipped cream to put between the biscuits

• Vigorously whisk the egg whites until they are so stiff that you can turn the bowl upside down.
• Stir in the icing sugar and hazelnuts.
• Drop round, quite large biscuits onto greased baking sheets.
• Bake at 100° for about 40 minutes.
• Sandwich the biscuits with whipped cream in the middle.

## Almond and orange stars
*(Makes about 18–20)*

400 g almond paste
2 egg whites
Grated peel of 1 orange

• Grate the almond paste and the orange peel on a grater. Mix with the egg whites, a little at a time. Work into a smooth and quite runny batter.
• Pipe out into stars: two triangles with about 6–7 cm long sides, placed on top of one another on a greased baking sheet.
• Bake the almond stars at 175° for about 12–15 minutes.
• If you want you can dip part of the star in melted cooking chocolate. Melt the chocolate in a bain-marie and dip half the star into it. Then leave to stiffen.

## Christmas stars
*(Makes about 18)*

*Puff pastry:*
*See the recipe for apple strudel on page 42 or use four sheets of frozen puff pastry.*

*Filling:*
1 1/2–2 dl raspberry jam

• Make the puff pastry according to the recipe, or defrost frozen puff pastry.
• Roll out the pastry into a large, thin rectangular sheet. Cut out 8 x 8 cm squares. Make a cut at each corner towards the middle, but not all the way in.
• Spoon in a blob of raspberry jam, and fold alternate flaps towards the middle. Press the edges together.
• Place the stars on cold baking sheets.
• Bake them at 225° for about 10 minutes.

## Lucia buns
*(Makes about 35)*

*One of my mother's old recipes.*

*Dough 1:*
50 g butter
5 dl milk
50 g fresh yeast
1 tsp salt
1 tbsp sugar
About 1 1/4 l flour

*Dough 2:*
1 g saffron
1 sugar lump
125 g butter
1 1/2 dl sugar
1 egg
About 5 dl flour

*To glaze and decorate:*
1 egg
Raisins

*Dough 1:*
• Melt the butter and pour in the milk. Heat to luke-warm. Dissolve the yeast in the liquid. Add sugar, salt and flour, a little at a time. Knead into a supple dough.
• Leave to rise for about one hour.

*Dough 2:*
• Crush the saffron and the sugar lump in a mortar. Cream the butter and sugar until white and porous. Add the egg and the saffron.
• Mix both doughs together and add the flour, a little at a time. Knead well. Form the Lucia buns into S-shapes with a long tail. Press a raisin into each end and place the Lucia buns on greased baking sheets. Leave to rise for 20 minutes. Brush with beaten egg.
• Bake at 225–250° for 7–9 minutes.

## Rosendal's ginger cake with lingonberry

*A very moist and spicy ginger cake. It also keeps very well. Use cranberries if you cannot get lingonberries.*

100 g butter
2 eggs
2 1/2 dl sugar
1 1/2 dl crème fraiche
1 1/2 tsp ground ginger
1 1/2 tsp ground cloves
1 1/2 tsp freshly crushed cardamom
2 tsp cinnamon
1 dl lingonberry or cranberry jam (not too sweet, prefer-ably raw-stirred)
1 tsp bicarbonate
About 3 1/2 dl flour

• Melt the butter and leave to cool somewhat.
• Whisk the egg and sugar until white and porous.
• Add the butter, crème fraiche, lingonberry or cran-berry and spices.
• Mix the bicarbonate into the flour and add to the cake mixture.
• Pour the mixture into a greased and breadcrumbed cake tin (about 1 1/2 litres).
• Bake the cake at 200° for about 45 minutes.

## Rosendal's Stollen

*(Two smaller cakes or one large)*
*What is a Christmas Fair without Stollen? This is a gen-erous, moist and somewhat spicy Stollen, that came about after trying endless variations! During the twelve days of the Christmas Fair we bake more than one thou-sand of these cakes! All the fruit is chopped by hand and left to soak in cognac.*

200 g figs
160 g apricots
2 3/4 dl sultanas
100–125 g candied orange peel
1 1/2 dl cognac
200 g butter
1 1/2 dl sugar
3 eggs
3 1/2–4 dl flour
1 tsp baking powder
1–2 tsp ground cinnamon
1–2 tsp ground cloves
1 tsp ground ginger

• Finely chop the fruit by hand. If you do it in a machine the fruit will get sticky. Mix all the fruit with the cognac and leave to stand overnight.
• Cream the butter until white and porous. Add the eggs, one at a time, and then the fruit mixture.
• Mix the flour with the spices and bicarbonate. Stir it into the batter and mix well.
• Spoon up the mixture into long cake tins, greased and breadcrumbed. For the smaller cakes use a one litre tin, for the larger cake a two litre tin. Leave the surface uneven, so that the cake will look more "lively" when it has been baked.
• Bake at 175° for about 45–55 minutes. Lower the heat towards the end if necessary. This cake keeps very well and almost tastes better the day after. Powder the cake with some icing sugar before serving.

## Rosendal's Panettone

*A cake I learned to love when I lived in Italy, where it is just as common as our cinnamon buns are in Sweden. I bake it for the Christmas Fair at Rosendal. It is not all that easy to succeed with, but with care and a place free from draughts for the cake to rise, it usually goes well. It takes a while to make, but all good thing's come to he who waits…*

5 dl flour
30 g fresh yeast
1 1/2 dl lukewarm milk
2 egg yolks, lightly whisked
1 egg
80 g butter
Scant 1 dl sugar
3 tbsp vanilla sugar
Grated peel of 1 orange
90 g sultanas
1/2–1 dl cognac

• Put the raisins in the cognac to soak for a few hours.
• Melt the butter and add milk. Heat to lukewarm.

Candied orange peel dipped in white and dark chocolate. *Page 186:* spiced sweet and sour oranges.
*Following spread:* in the background; spiced sweet and sour oranges, vanilla pears, saffron pears and lingonberry pears
(in jars), gingersnap vinegar (in bottles), Panettone, Stollen and star-shaped Lennart cake (in cellophane).
Back row; Christmas plate (meatballs, pâté pie, braised red cabbage, ham, beetroot salad and mustard-potato salad),
Dijon mustard with honey and thyme (in a jar), klenäter, Panettone, Stollen, ginger cake, Lucia buns,
saffron rusks (in a jar), and gingersnap dough. Middle row; liver pâté sandwich, kale soup, saffron and orange cake,
ginger nuts, almond moulds with cloudberry jam and cream, nut meringue sandwich with cream and gingersnaps.
Front row; white chocolate mousse gâteau, nut tart, Lennart cake, saffron rusks and saffron pudding.

- Pour the flour into a bowl and make a "hole" in the middle. Dissolve 1 tbsp sugar and the yeast in some lukewarm milk. Pour it into the "hole" and sprinkle with a little flour. After a while the mixture will bubble and rise to twice the size.
- Whisk the egg yolks and grate the orange peel.
- Mix all the ingredients while stirring, but not for too long or too vigorously.
- Pour out the dough into a special Panettone tin. This is a round tin with high edges and a hole in the middle. If you don't have a tin like this you can use an ordinary 1 1/2 litre wreath tin, but this doesn't have quite the right character.
- Leave the cake to rise in a place that is absolutely free from draughts for about 1–1 1/2 hours or until it is about 2 cm from the edge. (It will rise over the edge during baking.)
- Bake the cake at 175° for 40–50 minutes. Powder with icing sugar.

## Lennart cake

*This cake is called Lennart cake after a middle-aged gentleman who expressed his delight over the cake so vehemently that we named it after him. The cake is somewhat sticky in consistency, but so it should be!*

200 g butter
2 1/2 dl sugar
3 eggs
Peel and juice of 1 orange
5 tbsp candied orange peel
About 4 dl flour
1 tsp baking powder
80 g dark Belgian cooking chocolate

- Cream the butter and sugar until white and porous. Add the eggs, candied orange peel and the juice and grated peel of the orange.
- Mix the flour and the baking powder. Coarsely chop the chocolate. Flour lightly.
- Stir everything into the batter.
- Pour into a greased and breadcrumbed round, detachable cake tin (about 23 cm in diameter).
- Bake at 150° for about 40–45 minutes.
- Powder the cake with icing sugar. Sprinkle with grated orange peel and chocolate. Serve with whipped cream.

## Saffron and orange cake

200 g butter
1/2–1 g saffron
1 sugar lump
2 eggs
3 dl sugar
1 1/2 dl double cream
Peel and juice of 1 small orange
About 4 dl flour
2 tsp baking powder

- Melt the butter and leave to cool somewhat.
- Crush the saffron in a mortar together with the sugar lump.
- Whisk the egg and sugar until white and porous. Add the saffron, cream, butter and the grated peel and juice of the orange.
- Mix the flour with baking powder and stir into the batter. Pour into a greased and breadcrumbed tin (about 23 cm in diameter).
- Bake the cake at 175° for about 40 minutes. Serve newly baked, with a dollop of cream.

## Christmas sandwiches at the garden café

*As an extra Christmas attraction we increase our selection of open sandwiches during the Christmas Fair. Here are a few examples:*

- A generous slice of liver pâté on a lettuce leaf on dark bread spread with butter. Two slices of our own pickled beetroot are put on top as a crowning glory.
- Ham sandwiches of course. We have them the whole year round, but at Christmas we add a generous spoonful of our own beetroot salad.
- On the days when we have made "too many" meatballs for the Christmas buffet we use them to make a favourite open sandwich. The meatball sandwich is large and generous, and with mustard-potato and beetroot salad makes a whole meal.

## Beetroot salad

*(About 8–10 servings)*

About 15 pickled beetroot
1 red onion
2 apples
1 tbsp brown sugar
2–2 1/2 dl mayonnaise
2–2 1/2 dl crème fraiche
Salt to taste

- Coarsely chop the beetroot and finely chop the onion and apples. Mix the mayonnaise and crème fraiche, adding the brown sugar. Stir the mixture into the chopped beetroot, a little at a time, until the salad has the right consistency. Add more mayonnaise if necessary. Salt to taste.

## Braised red cabbage

*(About 8–10 servings)*

*Braised red cabbage tastes even better if it is made a few days before it is to be eaten.*

1 head red cabbage, about 1 kg
1 red onion, finely chopped
1 apple, finely chopped
50 g butter
3–4 tbsp of our gingersnap vinegar. You can also use another tasty vinegar.
1/2 litre red wine
3 dl stock or ham broth (not too salty)
4 whole cloves
3 allspice peppercorns
2 bay leaves
1 1/2 dl blackcurrant jelly
Salt to taste
Pepper

• Core the cabbage and slice finely. This is easiest to do with a cheese slicer. Finely chop the onion and apples.
• Melt the butter in a large pot. Fry the onion, apple and cabbage for 5–10 minutes, over a moderate heat.
• Mix in the other ingredients, except the jelly, salt and pepper.
• Simmer under a lid for about one hour until the liquid has boiled off.
• Add the jelly towards the end of the cooking time, and add salt and pepper to taste.

## Juicy meatballs

1 kg ground beef
1 1/2 dl breadcrumbs
2 dl dark beer, such as porter
1 dl double cream
2 tsp salt
2 tsp black pepper
2 tbsp Dijon mustard
1 red onion, chopped fine
1 egg
Butter for frying

• Mix all the liquid, and add the breadcrumbs. Stir in the spices and egg.
• Fry the onion in the butter in a frying pan.
• Mix everything with the ground beef.
• Shape into meatballs and fry them in butter.

## Pâté pie

*A simplified version of pâté. This is very juicy and somewhat spicy. It is excellent for freezing.*

500 g ground beef
1 red onion
4–5 large Estonian lactic-pickled gherkins (or some other sort of good, salty gherkin).
Some sun-dried tomatoes, bottled in oil. (Or oven-dried tomatoes bottled in oil. See recipe on page 161.)
2 eggs
2–3 dl double cream
1 tbsp potato flour
Salt
Coarsely ground black pepper

• Peel and finely chop the onion. Chop the gherkins and tomatoes into small pieces.
• Mix together all the ingredients and flavour with salt and pepper. Be careful with the salt, since the gherkins themselves are very salty.
• Pour into a well-greased dish of about 1 1/2 litres.
• Bake at 180–200° for about 50–60 minutes.

## Mustard-potato salad

*(About 8–10 servings)*

*We serve lots of different kinds of potato salad at the garden café. They are all inspired by the different seasons. This one is specially composed for our Christmas buffet. This is a white, smooth potato salad with a wonderful mustard flavour.*

16–20 potatoes
2–2 1/2 dl mayonnaise
2–2 1/2 dl crème fraiche
2–4 tbsp Dijon mustard
Capers
Black pepper

• Peel and divide the potatoes into smallish pieces. Boil in lightly salted water, until soft but still firm.
• Mix the mayonnaise and crème fraiche. Pour the mixture over the potatoes and stir in the desired amount of mustard.
• Add a few spoonfuls of capers and season with black pepper.

# Kale soup

*(About 4 servings)*

*Kale grows throughout the winter in our garden at Rosendal, and we pick it when we need it. Our guests are delighted when they see our well-wrapped gardeners come in with wheelbarrows full of kale and snow. We take the kale into the kitchen, clean, rinse and parboil it. Then we just have to transform the kale into this wonderful soup, flavoured with lots of thyme. A halved egg and a blob of crème fraiche help to lift the flavour when serving. We sometimes make it more Christmassy by colouring the crème fraiche red with some beetroot juice!*

3 tbsp butter
1 piece of leek
8 dl stock or ham broth (not too salty)
About 6 dl kale, fresh, parboiled and coarsely chopped
Salt
Pepper
Thyme
About 2 dl double cream

• Melt the butter in a cooking pot and fry the leek, sliced into fine strips.
• Add the stock, a little at a time. Boil for a couple of minutes.
• Add the fresh, parboiled kale and leave to boil for two minutes more.
• Flavour with salt (remember that if the stock is salty, you may not need more), pepper and lots of thyme.
• Finally mix in the cream.
• Serve with a halved egg and, if you like, some crème fraiche coloured red with beetroot juice.

# Saffron pudding

*This beautiful golden-yellow pudding is served in brown pottery bowls, for the enjoyment of young and old alike during the Christmas Fair.*

3 dl water
2 tbsp butter
2 dl round-grain rice
7 dl cream-milk (3 1/2 dl double cream and 3 1/2 dl milk)
1/2 tsp salt
About 2 tbsp sugar
1 g saffron
1 sugar lump

• Boil up the water and butter. Add the rice and salt. Stir and simmer on a low heat until the water is absorbed.
• Stir in the cream-milk and simmer the pudding on a low heat under a lid until it thickens. This takes about 35 minutes. If the pudding becomes too thick, just stir in more cream or milk.
• Crush the saffron and the sugar lump. Add this to the pudding and flavour with sugar to taste. Stir and serve the pudding with cold milk and cinnamon, if desired.

# Apple lollipops

*Red, shining and dipped in snowflakes, I mean coconut flakes. We do a roaring trade with these traditional Swedish apple "lollipops" at our Christmas Fair.*

5 small, undamaged Cox's Orange apples
3 dl sugar
1/4 dl water
Scant 1 tbsp glucose
5 drops red caramel colouring
5 short lollipop sticks
Desiccated coconut for dipping the lollipops in

• Polish the apples. Take away the stalk, and insert a lollipop stick into each apple.
• Boil the sugar, water and glucose vigorously. Stir occasionally.
• Test the sugar liquid by dipping a stick into it. The liquid should stiffen like glass. It should be breakable.
• Add the caramel colouring and stir.
• Dip the apples in the liquid and twirl around. Let them run off over the saucepan. Roll them in the desiccated coconut and stand on a baking sheet to cool.

# Chocolate truffle

*Our chocolate truffle has become an irresistible favourite at Christmas. It is also a greatly appreciated Christmas present!*

250 g dark Belgian cooking chocolate (or 250 g white Belgian chocolate)
200 g butter
2 dl icing sugar
A little grated orange peel
5 tbsp rum
4 tbsp cocoa. (Leave this out if you are using white chocolate. Use two spoonfuls of vanilla sugar instead.)

*For garnishing:*
Alternative 1 Cocoa
Alternative 2 Melted chocolate

• Melt the butter in a bain-marie. Leave to cool somewhat. Stir occasionally so that it does not form lumps.
• Cream the butter and sugar until porous. Mix it with the chocolate.
• Add the orange peel, cocoa (or vanilla sugar) and rum.
• Pipe the truffle onto grease-proof paper or roll small balls by hand. Leave to set in the fridge.
• Roll the truffles in cocoa or dip them in the melted chocolate (the white ones in dark chocolate, and the dark ones in white chocolate).

## SAFFRON AND ORANGE VINEGAR

*This vinegar glitters like gold as it stands in its bottles on our shelves. It is superb for using with carrots.*

1 l white wine vinegar
1 g saffron
1 orange

• Rinse the oranges and slice. Put the saffron and slices of orange in the vinegar and leave to draw in a warm, light place for about for weeks.
• Strain the vinegar and pour into an attractive bottle. Put in a couple of strips of orange peel, both for the extra taste and for decoration.

Candied clementines. *Previous spread:* Candied orange peel with aniseed stars.

## Candied orange peel dipped in white and dark chocolate

*Chocolate-dipped candied orange peel is a delicacy, both after a meal and with coffee. It is also a favourite on the Christmas table. It takes a few days to make and is a bit fiddly, but it is well worth it. It is especially important to use biodynamically grown oranges in this recipe, since we are using the peel.*

*Sugar liquid for 1/2 kg peel:*
8 dl sugar
3 dl water
Strained juice of 1 lemon

*For garnishing:*
About 75 g white and 75 g dark Belgian cooking chocolate for dipping the peels into.

• Peel the oranges and try to keep the peel as whole as possible. Put the peel in cold water for two days. Change the water occasionally.
• Place the peel in boiling water and let it boil until soft. Pour off the water and remove all the white pith with a small, sharp knife. Weigh the peel and slice into thin strips.
• Boil the ingredients to the sugar liquid. Put in the peel and lower the temperature. Let it simmer until the peel looks transparent. This takes about 50–70 minutes.
• Take out the peel with a perforated ladle and drain well.
• Melt the chocolate in a bain-marie, white chocolate in one and dark chocolate in the other. Dip the peel in the chocolate and lay on baking sheets covered with plastic cling film while setting. Keeps well if stored in a cool place.

## Gingersnap vinegar

*This vinegar has the scent and flavour of Christmas spices. It gives a characteristic taste to many vegetable dishes. Beautifully bottled, it has a given place on a shelf in the kitchen.*

1 l white wine vinegar
2 cinnamon sticks
A few cloves
A few cardamom kernels
1 piece ginger

• Put the whole spices into the vinegar and leave to stand and draw in a warm, light place for 4–5 weeks.
• Strain the vinegar and pour into an attractive bottle. Put some whole spices into the bottle if you wish.

## Rosendal's Dijon mustard with honey and thyme

*A very simple and tasty suggestion for making Dijon mustard taste home-made. We get both the honey and the thyme from our garden. Of course you can vary the flavouring according to your own taste.*

Dijon mustard
Honey to taste
Thyme to taste

• Heat the honey in a saucepan on a low heat. Stir with a wooden spoon until the honey has melted. Add the mustard. Flavour with lots of thyme.
• Pour the mustard into well-cleaned jars and seal. Store in a cool place.

## Spiced sweet-and-sour oranges
*(Two jars of 200 ml each)*

*These oranges are really good for using in woks, doing a roast or making sauces. They can be eaten as pickles and they are, moreover, beautiful to look at!*

4–5 oranges
3 dl white vinegar
4 1/2 dl sugar
3 cinnamon sticks, about 4 cm long
10–15 whole cloves

• Wash the oranges and cut them into thin slices straight over.
• Pour the vinegar, sugar and cinnamon sticks in a saucepan and simmer over a low heat. Stir occasionally until the sugar has melted.
• Add the sliced orange. Bring to the boil, then lower the heat and simmer the oranges for about an hour or two until the peel is transparent.
• Take two hot, well-cleaned glass jars of 200 ml each. Pack the oranges into the jars, with cloves and cinnamon.
• Boil up the sugar-liquid. Strain and pour into the jars so that it covers the slices of orange. Seal immediately.

## Candied orange peel with aniseed stars

*This orange peel can be used in baking, chopped fine and without the aniseed. It is fantastically good with ice cream. Try using it in cooking, too. It makes a beautiful present. The contents of these jars remind me of fishes and starfish.*

Oranges
Water

*Sugar liquid for 1/2 kg peel:*
3 dl water
8 dl sugar
Juice of 1 lemon, carefully strained and with all the fruit pulp removed
6–10 aniseed stars

• Peel the oranges and try to keep the peel as whole as possible. Put the peel in cold water for two days. Change the water occasionally. Bring the water to the boil in a saucepan, and put in the peel. Make sure there is enough water to cover the peel. Boil until soft.
• Take out the peel and drain. It is now easy to remove the white pith with a sharp knife. Weigh the peel and slice into the size you want: either finely chopped or in wider strips.
• Mix the ingredients for the sugar liquid. Boil up the liquid and put in the orange peel. Lower the heat and simmer until the peel looks transparent. This takes about an hour. When the peel is almost ready add the aniseed to simmer for the last ten minutes (the number of aniseed stars you use depends on how strong you want the flavour).
• Take out the peel and drain. Put the peel with the aniseed stars into hot, well-cleaned jars. Pour over the hot liquid and seal.

## Candied clementines

*You have to have a lot of creative energy and imagination when working with the Christmas Fair. Our own products – the preserves, the jams and all the home-made cakes – are the most sought after products at the Fair, and thus don't stay on the shelves for very long. New ideas and different taste combinations are tested with great care. The wonderful, attractive and delicious results decorate the shelves at the Fair the next day…*
*Clementines are eaten just as they are, with the peel and all. Make them a few days before they are to be eaten, so that they can stand and improve. They go well with whipped cream or full-cream ice.*

1 kg small clementines, biodynamically grown
2 dl sugar
2 cinnamon sticks
2 vanilla pods
2 1/2 dl water

• Rinse the clementines and prick the peel with a needle. Boil up the water and sugar. Stir until the sugar has dissolved.
• Split the vanilla pods and carefully scrape out the little black seeds. Put the vanilla pods and seeds, cinnamon and clementines in the sugar liquid and simmer together for about an hour. The fruit are ready when they look transparent.

• Take out the clementines and drain. Put them into hot, well-cleaned preserving jars. Strain the hot sugar liquid, pour it over the clementines and seal the jars.

## Saffron pears

*We have three different sorts of bottled pears at the Christmas Fair. These pears are a classic dessert, the bottles are decorative and together they make a nice Christmas present. Saffron pears are the most popular.*

2 kg pears
2 l water
1 3/4 l sugar
2 g saffron
1 lemon for lemon water

• Peel the pears, leaving the stalks intact. Put them into the lemon water so they do not go brown.
• Mix the water, sugar and saffron in a saucepan. Boil the liquid and stir until the sugar has dissolved.
• Put in the pears and boil them for 15–25 minutes. How long they need to boil depends on the size, ripeness and variety of pear. If you don't have room for them all at the same time in the saucepan, you can boil them in batches.
• If the pears are to be eaten later, preserve them in attractive bottles. See page 213.
• Serve with ice cream or whipped cream.

## Rosendal's lingonberry pears

*Deep-red, tangy and with a slight taste of cinnamon, these pears are my own favourite Christmas bottled pears. Use cranberry jam if you can't get lingonberry. Serve with whipped cream or creamy vanilla ice cream!*

4–5 large pears (about 1 kg)
4–5 dl lingonberry or cranberry jam
2 dl water
2 cinnamon sticks
A few whole cloves
2–4 dl sugar, the amount you use depends on how sweet the jam is.
1 lemon for lemon water

• Peel the pears, leaving the stalks intact. Put them into the lemon water so they do not go brown.
• Boil up the water, jam, sugar and spices. Put in the pears and boil them for 15–25 minutes depending on the size, ripeness and variety of pear. Stir carefully every so often so that the lingonberries don't stick to the bottom.
• If the pears are to be eaten later, preserve them in attractive bottles. See page 213.

Mimmi,

en människa värd att älska och beundra.

När jag ibland bara sitter och ser på henne,

det kan vara under en måltid bland vänner,

hon sitter med ett glas i handen, pratar ivrigt,

skrattar ofta... Eller när jag ser henme stå

i köket på Rosendal bland alla olivoljor,

mjölsäckar, mängder av doftande kryddor.

Hon står där och leder arbetet bland sina

flickor och pojkar. Hojtar:

- Naná, det ska vara mera vitlök här! Massor av

  vitlök!

Javisst...

När jag ser på henne så får hon mig ofta att tänka

på på allt det goda, det vackra i detta vårt

enda liv.

Hela hennes person, allt vad hon företar sig,

utstrålar liv, skönhet, enkelhet.

Det finns hos henme - hur ska jag säga? -

något rent... något klassiskt.

Jag tror att hon i ett tidigare liv (observera mot-

sägelsen!) har levt och verkat i något av de riktigt

gamla landskapen: Bretagne, Toscana, Provence...

Ja, hon borde kanske ha  en liten restaurang med

bageri i St Paul de Vence...

Men hon sitter inte i sjön, för hon både bor och

förestår ett café på Djurgården i Stockholm, en av

världens vackraste platser. Så det så!

## 2

Hon har en, som det verkar, medfödd utsökt smak.

(Varför föds vissa männskor med en utsökt smak?

 De flesta verkar dessutom komma från Italien.)

Och trots sin skönhet har hon också något enkelt,

lantligt, nästan "bondskt" över sitt sätt att leva,

sitt sätt att... att g e.

För vad som utmärker denna flicka är att hon

hela tiden g e r till oss andra, ger med glädje.

Inman hon blev en kökets mästarinna var hon dansös.

(Från balett till bulle, från dans till vetekrans)

och dansade i femton år till musik av Stravinskij,

Bernstein... ja, allt.

Ett åt dansade hon sig genom hela Italien, det

vackra Italien som hon älskar inte minst för dess

mat och dryck.

När vi är lediga reser vi ut i världen. För att

upptäcka, njuta, finna "maximalupplevelser".

När vi varit i New York och Hollywood har hon ibland

blivit tagen för "moviestar". Man förväxlar henne

bland annat med systrarna Hemingway. När någon ber

om en autograf skriver hon då ibland Muriel Heming-

way, kanske för att glädja någon eller också bara

på pin kiv.

Men hon kan också säga: "Nej, nej, jag är ingen

moviestar! Jag är bagare!"

"Are you a baker?" utropade en ung man i New York.

Men han ville ha hennes autograf ändå.

För, som han uttryckte det: "Ni är den vackraste

bagare jag sett i hela mitt liv."

När hon var liten, 4 år, på västkustön där hon

är född, tultade hon en dag upp till tanten i kiosken.

Där stod hon, naken och solbränd, och sträckte sig

på tå för att se alla gotter som låg på disken.

Plötsligt pekade hon med sitt lilla finger,

log med sin smilgrop (som finns kvar!)

och utbrast högt och ljudligt på göteborgska:

"Dek däl sel gött ut!"

Tanten kunde varken då eller under resten av sommaren
motstå denna charmmamöver. Så den lilla åt sig på

det sättet igenom alla gottsorter som fanns på disken.

"De däl sel gött ut!" Ja, på den vägen är det ju.

Men nu är det hon som dukar fram till oss.

Och det ser underbart gott ut. Eller hur?

Jag som skriver det här har den stora glädjen och lxck
sch och lyckan att leva med henne, denna den vackraste
bagaren som världen någonsin skådat.

Och jag lovar och svär att vägen till m i t t hjärta

inte gick via magen! Nej nej!

För när vi träffades och blev förälskade åt vi alltid

ute på restaurang. Så det så.

Men ni skulle bara veta vad jag får till middag ikväll!

Det är så lätt att älska henne.

Jag kallar henne för det mesta Mimmi.

Men hon heter förstås Monika.

Thommy Berggren

Good Advice
from the
Kitchen

Dr. Ch Em Hagdahl's "bible", *The Art and Science of Cookery*. For some reason this book has become very special for me.
Maybe because it has been a rich source of inspiration, but perhaps also because I am attracted
by the way the book came about: Hagdahl was asked by some ladies to collect the recipes they used which they
held in high esteem. Since he was a true gentleman who was brought up not to deny a lady anything, he took this assignment
with the utmost seriousness. Hagdahl sought assistance from some foreign writers and from well-known Swedish authorities.
He thought it was doubtful that the recipes would appeal to everybody's taste, opinions and habits, so he therefore asked
them all to make changes in the recipes to improve them and thus they became more adapted
to his own personal taste. Anyway, it is both instructive and entertaining to read his large, thick cookbook.

It is not entirely easy to give good advice and simple tips in a book such as this about the garden café at Rosendal, containing as it does everything from baking and cooking to preserving. One reason is that all recipes behave differently, not only when the cook is a different person, but also from day to day. It is also a fact that some days just aren't suitable for baking a certain kind of cake or for making jam at all. I can say this with great certainty, since I bake the same kind of cakes many times over during the year. They are never quite the same! Exactly what this depends on is a mystery, which many people have tried to fathom. You can read one theory in the *"Sowing and Harvesting Almanac"*. This tells us that on certain days baking bread is doomed to failure, depending on which phase the moon is in, if it is waxing or waning and if the influence of the planets is destructive or constructive. I won't go into how scientifically correct and proven this theory is. But sometimes it is really true! This can be comforting to know when you are standing there with your failed buns. Maybe this was a so-called "leaf day" which wasn't at all suitable for baking.

One thing I do know, however: that the art of baking and the art of cooking are crafts that require a sensitivity of hand. If your senses aren't open and committed to the work in hand anything can go wrong. Yes, imagination, inspiration and sensibility are important qualities for a baker.

Experience has given us a few well-tried rules that are worth following. Being very particular when choosing raw ingredients and partaking of the knowledge there is about the different kinds of wheat and sugar we have today are important building blocks for a successful result. I shall try as well as I can to give an account of my own experiences and of the knowledge I have accumulated through the years. It can perhaps be of good use when you are baking, cooking or making jam. But first I would like to cite Doctor Charles Emil Hagdahl's introduction to his classic work *The Art and Science of Cooking*.

"The Art of Cookery is based mainly on experiment. Every day should add to our knowledge, because it adds to our experience. Cookery is an art that cannot be learnt in one day, nor can it be learnt purely by reading one book on the subject: You cannot become an accomplished cook through reading alone, just as little as you can become an artist in any discipline without practical experience. All academic study must be combined with practice and in cooking a great deal of this practice is to be able to change the recipe according to circumstance. For it is clear that no book about cookery, however large or erudite, can suit its recipes to the requirements of every family, neither in terms of quantity or quality."

# Baking and cookery

## Flour

First a few words about flour, that most important of ingredients in all doughs. The choice of flour is crucial for the character of the bread or cake. There are many different kinds of flour nowadays, with different grades of milling, which you can choose from for baking. Plain wheat flour has very good baking qualities, since it has a high gluten content. Plain wheat flour makes yeasted dough light and supple. The finest and whitest of wheat flours is called wheatgerm flour. Wheatgerm flour is sifted flour from the kernel of the wheat grain and has a low milling grade. But there are coarser wheat flours with a higher milling grade. This kind of wheat flour is called, in Sweden, country wheat flour or wheat bread flour. This is a somewhat coarser flour that gives a rustic character to the bread and cakes. I use a flour with similar qualities called Saltåkvarn flour, which is a somewhat coarser biodynamically grown, high-protein wheat flour from Saltå mill, outside Stockholm. I use Saltå's flour in all the recipes if no other flour is specified. You can, of course, user a finer flour, but then you should increase the amount of flour somewhat.

Wholewheat flour (graham) is flour that has the hull, grain, and germ left, that is, a whole meal flour. This

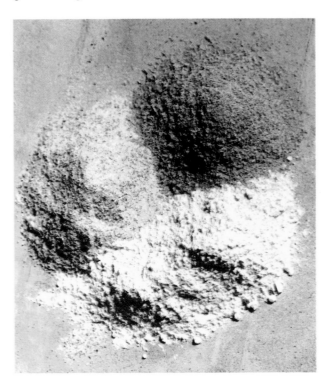

flour is mixed with sifted flour when baking to give it a good rising capacity.

Wheat bran is made of the thin hull or covering of the wheat grain. Wheat bran, like wheat germ and wheat flakes, is good and nutritious when used in home-made muesli or in baking.

Fine and coarse rye flour and rye flakes can be mixed with wheat flour in the dough to make tasty, coarser bread. Sifted rye flour is 40 per cent sifted rye flour and 60 per cent sifted wheat flour. The addition of wheat flour gives it better baking qualities.

Barley flour is mostly used with crispbread or porridge. It should be mixed with the wheat or rye flour for baking yeasted bread.

Oatmeal and oat flakes cannot be used by themselves in baking. But when they are mixed into a dough they give the bread a full and rich flavour.

## Sugar

Sugar is of great importance in baking with regard to consistency, colour and aroma. There are different kinds of sugar available. Granulated sugar, icing sugar, brown sugar and demerara sugar are examples of the different kinds of sugar I use in baking and preserving. Brown sugar gives a darker colour and a different taste. Dark brown sugar is used in our ginger biscuits. Demerara or unrefined sugar is heavier and fuller, and gives a special character to a cake. Sometimes I exchange the ordinary white sugar for demerara sugar with good results. It is important to use a little less sugar than usual in that case. You can also exchange the sugar for other sweeteners such as syrup and honey. Honey was used long before sugar. If you use honey, you should decrease the amount of liquid used, since honey contains water. You should also use a smaller amount, as with demerara sugar.

## Cooking fat

Butter and margarine are our most-used cooking fats. The vitamin content of butter varies according to the time of year, whereas in margarine it is always the same. Butter is churned from pasteurised, oxygenated cream. Butter gives bread and cakes an excellent flavour and fine moistness. Mankind has made butter for over 5000 years. Butter helps to emphasise the natural taste and aroma of the ingredients. I always use real butter, usually unsalted, and add salt to taste. The butter flavour comes out best in biscuits and cookies. Oil is better for some cakes or kinds of bread. Oil is 100 per cent fat. We get oil from the seeds and fruits of oil-yielding plants. I prefer to use a mild oil in baking, not olive oil, which has far too strong a taste. For deep-frying, it is best to use coconut oil.

## Spices

Spices are important! You get the best results from using whole herbs and spices that have been crushed in a mor-

tar or ground just before using. It may seem a bit complicated, but it is absolutely well worth the effort. Just think of the scent of newly ground cardamoms, so heavenly! A little salt will give your dough and batter a smooth texture and makes a yeasted dough easy to knead. The amounts of spices given in the recipes are average measurements and you can, of course, increase or decrease them according to your own taste. My rule of thumb is always that baking or cooking should have a full, rounded flavour. Too much salt or too hot spices shouldn't drown the taste. If the flavouring has become too strong, I often add a little cream.

## Seeds, flowers and fruit

Seeds such as sesame, poppy or sunflower add not only a decorative touch, but also a fine flavour. Dried flowers, nettles, the peel and juice of fruit are further examples of additives that not only give extra flavour but also have nutritional value. Be careful to brush the peel of citrus fruit very carefully in warm water before using. The very best thing is to do as we do at Rosendal: use only biodynamically grown fruit that are totally unsprayed. Always try to use only the outer layer of the peel since the inner, white part gives a bitter taste.

## Nuts

Nuts should always be fresh. There's a great difference between fine, fresh walnuts and those that have gone a bit old and dry. All nuts contain a lot of fat and should therefore be stored cool, or else they will go rancid.

When using all kinds of flavour-additives such as nuts, spices and fruit it is important to use ingredients of high quality. Experience has shown me that it is always best to be critical and inspect all the ingredients before starting to bake, make jam or cook. Afterwards it's too late, if the results don't live up to expectation.

Another thing that should be obvious is to read through the whole recipe before starting. This is of special importance in this book since the oven temperature is always given at the end of the recipe. It is important that the oven be well, and evenly, heated before putting things in. Another reason is that there might be an unusual ingredient that isn't usually used in a similar cake, so that you might not have it at home. Baking times vary from oven to oven, as do the temperatures. It is important, therefore, to check the oven every now and then so that nothing gets burnt, particularly on the first baking.

My biscuits and cookies are usually quite large, which is why the amounts given can seem a bit misleading. In these cases do, of course, as you yourself wish. Round baking tins with a hole in the middle bake quicker than long or round tins without a hole. Most of the recipes in this book are calculated for tins or rings of one and a half litres or 22–24 cm in diameter if nothing else is specified.

The size is right if the batter mixture fills the cake tin two-thirds full, not more! Be generous with butter when greasing a tin. You can leave out the breadcrumbs or replace them with desiccated coconut, poppyseed, chopped nuts or wheat bran.

If a cake looks ready but is soggy in the middle, then you can lower the heat somewhat and move it down to the bottom rung of the oven. It's a good idea to cover the cake with foil so that it doesn't go dry. Cakes are ready when a skewer can be put into them and pulled out with nothing sticking to it.

It is easier to handle a pastry that is going to be rolled out or cut up, if it has stood cold for a while.

You don't have enough baking sheets? Then place all the cakes or biscuits on greased-proof paper. This makes it easy to move them onto the baking sheet.

Attach the pastry to the edge of the tart or flan ring with aluminium foil before baking blind, or else it will slide down and the sides be lost. You can always save the foil until the next time you bake pastry! And don't forget to prick the bottom with a fork or similar, otherwise it will rise and make it difficult to get the filling in.

Mixers are used a lot these days, and it is important not to over-work the cake mixtures or yeasted doughs. Using an electric whisk, it takes about three minutes for a mixture of egg and sugar to be white and fluffy. Three to five minutes is enough for kneading a yeasted dough in a mixer.

You get a more tender and lighter bread or cake the less flour you have in the dough or batter. Therefore you should always add the flour a little at a time, starting with the smaller amount. It's always easy to add a little more if necessary. If you have nevertheless, too much flour, you can remedy this by working in a little more fat. Always measure the flour in a measuring jug, without packing it down.

Fresh yeast should be dissolved in lukewarm liquid, that is, 37°.

Push a hole in the dough with your finger. If the hole disappears fast, then the dough has risen enough. If the dough has been left to rise for too long and gone flat, you can always re-do it. Remove from the baking-sheet, knead and shape the dough again.

Yeasted bread will be light and airy and rise well, if it is put in a hot oven and the temperature immediately lowered by 25–50°. The loaf is ready if it feels light and sounds hollow when you tap it underneath. You can make the crust hard and crispy by brushing with water instead of egg, and if you leave the bread to cool without a cloth. If I want a moist loaf with a soft crust, then I wrap it in one or two towels and let it cool slowly.

You can freeze bread and cakes in plastic bags with the excess air squeezed out. Biscuits can be frozen in containers. How long frozen bread and cake will keep varies, those with a lot of fat in keep the worst.

Before I move on to processing and preserving I will just say a word about the measurements used in these recipes. In my own baking, I often use the old, well-tried measurements such as handful and pinch. You learn to see and judge these things through experience. In these recipes, however, I use recognised measurements. It is usually quicker to measure than to weigh ingredients, and often there aren't any scales in the house.

tsp = teaspoon
tbsp = tablespoon
dl = decilitre
l = litre
g = gram
kg = kilo
cup = coffee cup

Note that all temperatures are given in Centigrade.

# Processing and preserving

## Utensils

When making jam, jelly and fruit-syrup, it is practical to have all the utensils to hand. A large cooking pot of about ten litres with a thick, ground level bottom is a good investment. Wooden spoons for stirring, a long-handled perforated ladle for skimming the surface and funnels of differing widths for use when pouring are all extremely useful when making preserves. You also need a straining-cloth and stand when making fruit-syrup or jelly.

You can use most kinds of bottles and jars. A dark bottle will preserve the colour and vitamin content of summer fruit-syrup better than a clear one will. I use jars with screw tops and Kilner jars, or similar, that are sealed using rubber rings and metal clasps, for jam, marmalade and preserves.

## Sterilising and sealing

Irrespective of which kinds of jars and bottles you choose, it is important to sterilise them and seal well in order to achieve a good result. Wash the jars and bottles carefully in boiling hot water. Stand them upside down to dry. Place the bottles and jars in the oven and heat to 100°. The jars should still be hot when you pour in the jam. Screw the tops on the jars when the jam is still steaming hot. The same applies for Kilner jars with clasps and rubber rings and also for bottles with caps or corks. Put the rubber rings into boiling water and leave for about ten minutes. You can also put the corks into boiling water for a few minutes in order to soften them. Them press them firmly into the neck of the bottle.

Jam and jelly can also be paraffined. Melt the paraffin in a pan in a bain-marie. Pour the paraffin over the jam or marmalade when it has cooled, placing a piece of folded thread or string in it so you can easily lift out the paraffin when you open the jam. Cover the jars with paper, preferably greaseproof, and tie with string.

Hermetic sealing is the method we use at Rosendal. It is also the method that is best suited for conserving, pears for example. Use Kilner jars with clasps and rubber rings. At Rosendal we can seal hermetically in the oven, since we have an oven with a steam programme that you can boil in. The easy way to seal hermetically at home is to use a large pot on the cooker. First sterilise the jars as usual in the oven. Then fill the pot with water and place the jars in the pot. The water should cover the jars while

In the background: straining cloth, bottles, mixer, balloon whisk and wooden ladle (in the bowl) and jam-cooking pot. Back row: conserving jars, Panettone tin, litre measuring jug, Stollen tin, grater, mortar, nut grinder, and funnel. Middle row: rolling pin, bottle corks and jar lids, muffin tin, cake tins, pastry scraper, perforated ladle and scoop. Front row: wire sieve, peg rolling pin, citrus juicer, pastry cutter, cookie cutter, brush and apple peeler & apple slicer.

213

it is being heated. Heat to 60–70° for about 25 minutes. Let the jars cool slowly in the water. For long shelf life, store the conserves in a cool place.

Whatever method you use, it is important to skim well before pouring up the jam. Remove all the foam with a perforated ladle and leave the jam to rest for a couple of minutes.

## Ingredients

Fruit and berries that are to be processed must be of the best quality. It is an advantage if they are not quite ripe, since the pectin content is higher. This is especially important when making jam or marmalade. You test the consistency by using the so-called jam test. Pour a little jam on to a plate and leave to cool for a few minutes. Draw a line through the jam. If the line remains, then the jam is ready.

It can sometimes be difficult to get the right consistency for jam or marmalade. One trick is to add lemon peel and lemon juice or unripe apple halves that are put in to boil for a while. Another device is to add pectin, preferably home-made so that you avoid unnecessary additives. Home-made pectin is easy to make and keeps for several months in the fridge.

## Pectin

1 kg firm, unripe apples
1/2 l water

• Boil up the water and fruit. Simmer for 1–1/2 hours on a low heat until the fruit is completely soft. Test the pectin by pouring out some of the juice into a bowl. Add a couple of teaspoons of spirits. Shake the bowl carefully and leave to stand for a minute or so. If a lump of jelly forms, the pectin is ready. Otherwise leave to boil a little longer.

• Strain the juice and pour into hot, sterilised jars and seal.

• For jam or marmalade use 1 1/2–2 dl home-made pectin for 1 kg berries or fruit.

Berries should be rinsed only if absolutely necessary, and in which case quickly under cold water. Leave them to drain well. Pick over the berries carefully! Poorly cleaned berries never give good jam.

It is important to add enough sugar if the jam, fruit-syrup, marmalade or jelly is to keep well without using preserving agents. Sugar has a preserving effect. You should use at least 8 dl sugar per kilo of berries or fruit. (1 kg sugar = 1,2 litres sugar, 2 litres berries, for example raspberries, blueberries = 1 kilo berries). Keep the jars and bottles in a cool dark place to keep well without unnecessary preserving additives.

Sugar is of great importance even when pickling. The sugar prevents the cells of the vegetables from being broken down and keeps the contents fresh and full of taste and colour.

For preserved pears, apples, tomatoes and other fruit and vegetables use only firm, undamaged fruit. Remove squashed or bruised parts.

Peel the fruit and put them into cold water with the juice of two squeezed lemons, so that they do not go brown.

Carefully rinse and dry vegetables. Peel or top-and-tail according to the desired recipe.

You can make jam, marmalade and preserves during a large part of the year according to the different seasons for the berries, fruit and vegetables. It's always fun to be able to serve home-made produce. You always get a good result if you use top quality ingredients, if the jars and bottles are sterilised and if you work with care. Hand-written labels will add a personal touch to your jars of preserves.

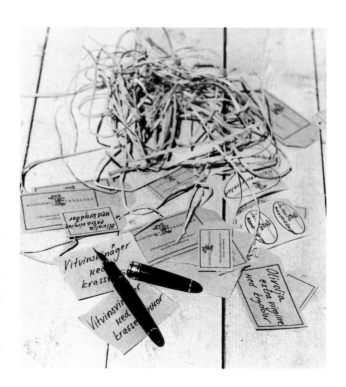

Good Advice
from the Garden

# The onion sets come first

*by*
*Malin Löfstrand, master gardener*

This is not a chapter about the Art of Cultivation. See it rather as a stroll through some of the crops in the garden, stopping here and there for a little story, edged with a few tips on what you can take back with you into the kitchen.

Our vegetables all have their own places out in the field. Side by side, row after row, composed so as to be both beautiful to look at and wholesome to eat. Crops such as leek, parsley, cabbage and lettuce are precultivated in the greenhouse during March and April, a task that characterises a large part of our spring labours. The packing-hall is filled, sometimes for several days on end, with our permanent employees, trainees and volunteers in order to prick out the thousands of quickly growing seedlings in time. After transplanting from the seed boxes to the individual pots, the plants are left to develop a good head of leaves and a sturdy, healthy root system. Then they are moved into the shade of the cold frames for hardening before they are ready to plant outside. After that, the work begins in the field.

The onion sets come first. You can even sow onions directly as seeds, but I prefer to plant ready-developed small onion bulbs. This means you can avoid all the work of thinning out and you can harvest spring onions already by the end of June. The onions that are meant for winter storing are left to wither out in the field before they are taken in to a dry, warm place. When the onions have dried, the remains of the leaves and the soil are brushed off, and they are packed into sacks for storing in cool and dry conditions.

Then it's time to plant out many other seedlings in long rows. Pricking out cabbage plants is a very special experience. With their large, blue-green leaves the plants display the many different ways there are of being a cabbage: broccoli, cauliflower, white and red cabbage, savoy and kale. When they have been planted out in May, and then watered, weeded and re-weeded they respond with heavy heads of leaves or flowers. A couple of rows of marigold flame up beautifully against the cabbages. We use them not only in our own tea-mixture but also to decorate the cakes when they are on display in the café.

We grow whole fields of different kinds of lettuce for the never-ending needs of the café. We have to remember, therefore, about every tenth day, to sow a box of lettuce: chicory, cos, radicchio or iceberg. With the same interval, we fertilise, water and zealously weed.

We plant onions next to the carrots, since the dreaded carrot fly hates their smell. Further on we plant beetroot, mangold, black salsify, swedes and more. We anxiously inspect the rows every day to see if the seeds have germinated. Phew! What a relief, the sowing has succeeded! Now it's time for that great trial: thinning out. Brandishing our hoes, we just have to plunge into one of the rows and get started. From that day onward all we can see are garden workers crawling along the rows, engaged in this appallingly meticulous occupation.

How on earth could I ever have thought of becoming a gardener? But after the thinning out, watering, weeding and re-weeding it begins to pay off. The carrots can be harvested in generous bunches for use in carrot cakes, or else taken up later in December for use during the winter.

Zucchini or courgettes have their place in the most fertile part of the field. They manage in one season to grow into bush-like plants with large lobate leaves. Their warm yellow flowers shine against the dark soil. The female flowers then develop into green, yellow or almost white fruit. The male flowers with their long stalks can be deep-fried in oil or used to decorate the table.

At the same time as we are hectically engaged in transplanting, there are other things to be done in the garden. One such big project is the large glasshouse that has stood empty since the Christmas Fair and which must be prepared for growing tomatoes. We make up beds of straw bales that are then filled with soil, turf and lots of well-decomposed compost. This can be a really sweaty job since the glasshouse is almost unendurable when the sun is shining. We transplant the tomato seedlings from their pots to these beds. They are trained on to strings hanging from the roof, to ensure that the plants don't get broken off or start to roam the glasshouse on their own. These plants require constant attention throughout the whole growing season until October to help them keep climbing. They have to be weeded and the plants must be "de-thieved" regularly. The "thieves" are side-shoots that grow out from the main stem and steal both sunlight and nutrition. When you are doing this job your fingers look as if they are covered in green oil paint that has been left to crack, the sap is that strong and intense. But certainly sun-warm, ripe and sweet tomatoes are really something!

Tomatoes and basil are a veritable mutual couple, both in cultivation and in cooking. I know this well, since it is sometimes difficult to satiate the café's constant appetite for this robust and musty herb. We grow it in the glasshouse since it hates strong sunlight and is frightened of wind and rain. It feels most at home indoors and well sheltered. We plant it in seed-beds with rich soil, on tables. When the plant has grown somewhat, we top it above the leaf pairs again and again. Finally it looks like a well-branched bush.

When the very first lettuce, the first spinach and the first radishes are being harvested in the glasshouse and the work has begun in the field, something begins to stir. Large, almost fleshy knobs begin to rise from the ground. These are the tightly wrapped rhubarb leaves that make their presence known in the warmth of spring, they look almost like living monsters. Soon they will stretch themselves out and the tender stalks can be picked. I hold the base of the stalk firmly and pull lightly to remove it without damaging the plant. I remember as children we used to dip the stalks in sugar and eat them like lollipops. I think the feeling was better than the taste. We pulled faces between chews, stubbornly assuring granny meanwhile that they tasted so good.

You can usually pick rhubarb up until Midsummer. Thereafter they send their massive flower stems skywards, and the stalks become woody and full of tannic acid.

When July comes around we get the same question from both the bakery and the kitchen: are the currants coming on? Aren't the currants ripe yet? Oh yes, comes the joyous reply from the garden, but also with a sigh, there's just so much to do.

The currant bushes grow in a sunny place where there is least risk for night frost. They are protected from the harsher winds by a dense hedge of rugosa rose. The berries hang in black, shining clusters, responding to the pruning of last autumn with an abundant crop. I sit on a stool with the pail between my knees and let the first cluster go right into my mouth! Mmmm... But from now on I must concentrate on picking, and not be too tempted by these delicacies. I pick the berries one by one and let them fall into the pail. This way you don't have to pick them over, and the unripe berries can be left for a later picking. When the berry picking is finished for this time, they are taken into the kitchen to be made into jam or put into tarts. Those that aren't used directly, are packed into boxes and put in the freezer.

We usually call our garden-patch the allotment. This is the little garden inside the big one. Thommy, our master gardener of the allotment, makes sure to have those delicacies that the big garden can't have. That is, raspberries and strawberries.

When I'm in the strawberry patch, it is easy to travel back in time to childhood summers at granny and granddad's house in the country with, as it seemed at the time, those endless rows of berries. Children and grandchildren alike had to help look after the strawberry patches. Weeding, removing runners and watering were some of the jobs on the list of work. The strawberries were to have just enough water before fruit-setting, a lot when the fruit were forming and then more sparsely when they were ripening. Our joy was total when granddad plodded up the slope with the first ripe strawberries, warmed by the sun, in his callused hands. They were served with newly skimmed cream...

Strawberries are best when freshly picked. If they are kept in a fridge, take them out in good time before serving since the cold dissipates their taste. If you take them from the freezer, they should be eaten almost frozen. They easily go a little grey and taste watery when defrosted.

The second year raspberry shoots stand at rigid attention, tied up with twine so as not to bend. The berries are picked in succession from the end of July to the beginning of August. They should be picked when red and ripe but still firm, so as not to crush them. It is best to pick them in dry weather, since they otherwise have a tendency to go mouldy. Raspberries are amongst the fruit that are excellent to freeze. Pack them into cartons. If, in spite of your care, they are somewhat crushed, freeze them on a tray before packing so they do not stick together. If you serve them straight after defrosting, they retain their fine aroma.

The herbs are grown in a sunny, dry but properly fertilised place where they collect their different taste sensations. Some are perennial, for example, sage with its thick grey-green leaves and blue or pink flowers. Oregano forms a thick, low cushion of dark green leaves. They flower too, in the late summer, with violet flowers. Lovage rises high above the ground, and shows off its large, aromatic leaves.

Some herbs are annual, for example marjoram with its soft, light green leaves which go so well in pea soup, or summer savory with its thin, mild flavoured leaves that can be used in white sauce.

The thyme plant appears to be somewhat fragile. In the spring, its dry, woody branches look as if they have

succumbed to winter's ferocity. And I am just as often pleasantly surprised when I see new, healthy, fragrant shoots emerging in the spring warmth.

The lavender plant with its grey-green leaves and violet flowers on their fragile stalks, have a tougher time in our climate. But if you plant them in a sunny, sheltered place they can nevertheless grow into small bushes.

I sow the herbs and spices both in the autumn and spring. Spring sowing gives us large plants for the plant shop during the autumn. Sowing in the autumn gives the plants time to develop for transplanting in May. Herbs and spices are wonderful when fresh, but they can also give much joy to cooking during the winter. I take out my secateurs, basket and raffia on a dry, sunny day in the early summer and step out into the herb garden. There I cut and bind bunches that are then left to hang in the attic where it is dry. A lot of these bouquets end up in the Christmas Fair, in beautiful bottles filled with vinegar or virgin olive oil.

The names found on our apple trees sound as if they have come out of a novel: Kalmar Glass, Golden Hook Astrakan, Ingrid Marie and Virginal Rose Apple. The beautiful, golden yellow Phillipa hangs under a umbrella of branches. The large, sturdy Åkerö apple tree stretches its branches straight up to the sky in its eager-

ness to catch the sun as a collaborator for giving colour and flavour to its fruit. The soil, warmth, and water work together to give us endless varieties of fruit. The skins can be shiny, waxy or dry and the colourings can vary from the lightest yellow to the deepest red, sometimes veering towards russet.

The branches are always ageing, but with the gardeners' help, the youngsters, the young branches, soon learn the rules and are trained in preparation for taking over from the old timers.

The pears are next door neighbours to the apples. It always seems to me as if Lord Esperen is nodding a greeting to Miss Herzogin Elsa, while the grey pears are deep in admiration of Louise d'Avranche's ruddy apparel. The Spring costumes, white clusters of almost erect blossom, are exchanged for new autumn creations. Warm-red and green are the most favoured colours, and they also feature one or two leather accessories. The flesh of the fruit is juicy, sweet and smooth.

A lot of Rosendal's apples are late autumn and winter varieties, many of which are suitable for storing right up until February. That is why we don't pick them until October, but before the frost. Fruit-picking is a time-consuming task, not least because the fruit must be picked carefully so as not to damage their fragile skin and flesh. The seventh-grade pupils from Martin's School always come for work experience one week every October. We usually get them to help us with both the fruit and the vegetable harvest. Ladders, baskets and fruit boxes are to be seen under every tree, and hubbub, laughter and groans can be heard from their crowns. The fruit is stored for as long as is possible in crates, well packed under blankets and tarpaulins. When Jack Frost makes his grand entry into the garden, the fruit together with the vegetables are moved into the earth cellar to be stored for later enjoyment during the long, dark winter months.

The place I stayed at as a child was called Fredsborg. It was inhabited primarily by my grandmother, thereafter her three daughters. The oldest was my mother, with her husband and two children, my sister Agneta and I. Fredsborg was a few kilometres from Åkers Runö station on the Roslags line.

The basket maker came at the beginning of summer. He came on his bike up the road to my mother's house – it was scattered with pebble-stone and red feldspar – and took her orders. And my grandmother did order, she came from the country, from Kalmar way, and was used to travelling craftsmen. Then he sat under the big oak tree by the gate, looked in his big sack with its sawdust and willow branches and began to plait the baskets that grandmother wanted.

We, my cousin and I, sat in the grass and watched his nimble fingers at work. In the afternoon, grandmother came out with coffee and sandwiches for all three.

Fredsborg had a large orchard, with apples, pears, cherries and strawberries. A few days after the basket-maker's visit it was time for the currant harvest. This annual ceremony was soon followed by another.

Red and blackcurrants with twigs, leaves and all were tipped into large, deep pans and boiled with a splash of water until they split.

Then the boiled mass was poured into large white cones (of tulle?) that were tied to the legs of upside-down chairs. Large bowls were placed underneath to catch the delicious drops of juice.

Anyone who has been in a house where moonshine is in preparation knows the sound.

I see before me a dozen white cones and hear the discreet dripping:

DRIP DROP DRIP DROP DROP DROP

When the juice was ready we had a blackcurrant party in the arbour with newly baked buns and cakes.

It was summer in August 1942. The war went on and the nights got darker and darker.

*Lars Forssell*

Loaf sugar! I forgot the loaf sugar that was used to sweeten the juice. Can you still buy them; those cones of sugar wrapped in coarse, white paper widening like pineapple slices, larger and larger down to the base?

Strawberries, Indians and other things

In those days we had all sorts of berries, rhubarb and fruit trees in our field. The woods were full of blueberries and lingonberries and you could pick all sorts of flowers in the meadow. Not only cowslips, meadow saxifrage, cat's-foot and violets, as it says in the Swedish song, but also even oxeye daisies, buttercups, bluebells, clover, and cornflowers. Potatoes, radish, lettuce and carrots were grown in straight rows.

Mother had "green fingers". She was probably most keen on her rose beds round the cottage, but anything that could be grown in the garden was important for the household in those days. You could enjoy lettuce, tomatoes, fresh berries and fruit during the season, wild strawberries grew on the south slope of the ditch by the road and poppies lit up the cornfield on the other side. Once I was almost decapitated by the harvester as I lay on my back examining an ear of wheat in the rustling, sundrenched cornfield. The farmer didn't see me, but the horse pulled up short.

My favourites were strawberries and raspberries and, towards the end of the summer, the yellow plums were exciting, although the cherries were more fun to pinch from Höl's farm. They had bigger trees that you could climb in. The farmer fired off his shotgun a few times, but looking back, I don't think he aimed at anything other than the stars, because I was never "scorched on the bum".

Our garden plots weren't just there for harvesting, but had to be dug and weeded as well.

I was just as invisible at weeding time as I was visible at harvest time. A lot of watering had to be done, but the well was a long way off, so if mother shouted with a bucket in her hand I was engulfed by Mother Nature, often hiding in a nearby sand quarry. This disused quarry had been transformed into a real Wild West through the years, the sparsely overgrown sand holes and ridges were ideal for an ambush. We played "cowboys and Indians" there in the shadow of the real war.

But back to the garden and our field. When my mother finally caught me, I occasionally had to use my paws to weed the strawberry patch.

Our own strawberries were, of course, the best, but the ones from Möja were sweeter and better for jam and juice.

The dark red Möja strawberries arrived on open, tarred boats down in our creek and were brought up in triumph to the cottage.

The surrounding trees and bushes were soon shrouded in the heavenly aroma of that year's jam cooking.

The steam from pans on the wood-fired stove stole out through the open kitchen window and was caught up by the warm evening breeze. When this smell reached the "Wild West", the quarry that is, all Indian warfare ceased, and the combatants who had been magically transformed into extremely helpful hands, were suddenly to be found sitting side by side in the diningroom, mashing the Möja strawberries with the cream from the milk churn they had so quickly and willingly lugged home from the farm.

Thus could a summer evening draw to a close, in the days when we had berries and flowers and fruit-trees in our field.

*Sven-Bertil Taube*

Your tiger cake tastes
ten times better than mum's!
(but don't tell mum!)

*Henry B.*

Lennart cake

A somewhat heavy cake, but well balanced, with the consistency and a certain aroma of clay soil in the spring. Its long aftertaste contains a bitter fruitiness that arouses associations with Christmas and mulled wine.

This cake tastes best after a meal with game, such as roast hare with chanterelles and lingonberry. Eat it preferably with a cup of strong coffee with hot milk, or possibly a double expresso. With its roots in the Swedish soil, this cake continues a long tradition from the old Swedish inns.

*Lennart Winqvist*

Dear Monika,
if a kitchen doesn't smell of garlic, it isn't a proper kitchen!

That's what one of my friends usually says when she comes into mine. When I tasted Your salt-baked, oven-baked, magnificent garlic I was left with no peace of mind until I had made some myself.

So now my kitchen smells even stronger (worse, someone said).

It's so seldom that a dish combines such a rustically attractive taste and appearance! You eat for others as well! So – don't forget that little English verse:

*But lest your kissing should*
*be spoilt*
*Your Onion must be thorough*
*boil'd!*

*Your friend Hiram*

You make it look good and taste good!

*Peter Dahl*

Siena cake

The sweet of the icing sugar and almond mixes with the bitter taste of the orange peel. The white filmy powder floats like a haze down on to the knees of my black dress, while I look out over the garden at Rosendal.

*Pottery maker*
*Ingegerd Råman*

Path to Happiness
Song for Monika
By Yngve Gåsöj

For a long time I used to think
that Happiness was a Song,
of Life's delight and love,
yes, Life in joyous capers.

But in spite of all my searching
that Happiness I never found.
Until I came to Rosendal's café,
and my fears did melt away.

She stood at proud attention,
with flour on her brow, nose, throat.
Holding forth her baking splendours.
My heart struck up a waltz.

Suddenly I could clearly see
how wrong I'd been before.
For, Happiness is Carrot Cake,
that Monika has baked.

Fårö 11.5.94
Dear Monica!

You rang and asked me to write something about wild strawberries. It will be both a short and a sad story. I have been allergic to wild strawberries all my life. Five wild strawberries are all right. But if I sin and eat seven, then I am afflicted by small firey red, madly itching rashes round my wrists and ankles. Sometimes – very rarely – I really indulge. In the woods behind my house there is a field. It is reddened with wild strawberries several times during the summer, big heavy fragrant wild forest-strawberries, it's like a miracle and I indulge without a thought for the consequences, which promptly make themselves known. Yes, it is terrible and typically Bergman-like but I console myself; the smell of newly picked wild strawberies is like special music, it gives me a concrete conception of paradise, infinity – perfection. I don't really know how I can put this, it sounds far too grand, but I can't find any other words so it will have to be like this.

*Fondest regards*
*Ingmar*

Sun-dried tomatoes

First find nothing
Out of nothing make everything
Out of everything make energy
Out of energy create a world
In this world place a
TOMATO

Fifteen billion years of preparation
About ten minutes from town
...if you walk

*Mikael Rundquist*

Mimmi,
a person worthy of love and admiration. Sometimes when I am just sitting and looking at her, it can be during a dinner party with friends, she's sitting with a glass in her hand, talking eagerly, laughing often… Or when I see her standing in the kitchen at Rosendal amongst all the olive oils, flour sacks, a multitude of fragrant spices. She stands there leading the work amongst her boys and girls. She shouts:

"Naná, we need more garlic here! Lots of garlic!"

To be sure…

When I look at her she often makes me think of all the good things, the beautiful things in this our one and only life.

Her whole person, everything she does, radiates life, beauty, simplicity.

She possesses – how should I put it? – something pure… something classical.

I think that in an earlier life (note the contradiction!) she has lived and worked in one of the really old landscapes: Brittany, Tuscany, Provence… Yes, maybe she should have a little restaurant and bakery in St Paul de Vence…

But she's not badly off, since she both runs a café and lives on Djurgården in Stockholm, one of the most beautiful places in the world. So there!

She has, so it seems, an inborn exquisite taste. (Why are some people born with good taste? Most of them seem, moreover, to come from Italy.) In spite of her beauty there is something simple, rural, almost "rustic" about her way of living, her way of… giving.

For that which distinguishes this girl is that she is always giving to the rest of us, giving with joy. Before she became a mistress of the kitchen she was a dancer. (From ballet to bun, from dance to dough) and danced for fifteen years to the music of Stravinskij, Bernstein… yes, everything.

One year she danced through the whole of Italy, the beautiful Italy she loves, not least for its food and drink. In our spare time, we travel the world. To discover, enjoy, to find those "maximum experiences". Occasionally when we have been in New York or Hollywood, she's been mis-

taken for a "moviestar". They confuse her, amongst other things, with the Hemingway sisters. When someone asks for an autograph, she sometimes writes Muriel Hemingway, maybe to please someone or maybe just to tease.

But she can also say: "No, no, I'm not a moviestar! I'm a baker!"

"Are *you* a baker?" exclaimed a young man in New York. But he wanted her autograph anyway.

Since, as he put it: "You are the most beautiful baker I've seen in my whole life."

When she was little, 4 years old, on the island off the West Coast of Sweden, where she was born, she toddled up to the lady in the kiosk. There she was, naked and sunburnt, and stretching up to see all the goodies on the counter. Suddenly she pointed with her little finger, smiled with her dimple (which is still there!) and exclaimed loud and clear in her Gothenburg dialect:

"Dat looks good!"

The kiosk lady couldn't resist this charming manoeuvre, neither then nor during the rest of the summer. So, in this way, the little one ate her way through the whole assortment of sweets. "Dat looks good!" Yes, that's the way it is. But now it is she who puts the goodies on the table. And it looks wonderful, too. Doesn't it?

I, the writer of this piece, have the great joy and happiness of living with her, this, the most beautiful baker the world has ever seen.

And I can honestly swear to you that the way to my heart didn't go through my stomach! No no!

For when we meet and fell in love, we always ate at restaurants. So there.

But if you only knew what we're having for dinner this evening!

It is so easy to love her.

I usually call her Mimmi.

But her name, of course, is Monika.

*Thommy Berggren*

Essays

Lars Forssell/author
Sven-Bertil Taube/singer and actor
Henry Bronett/circus manager
Lennart Winqvist/executive
Kent Andersson/author and actor
Ingegerd Råman/potter
Ingmar Bergman/film director
Yngve Gåsöy/musical artist
Charlotta Åkerblom/café girl and art student
Märit Huldt/food writer
Peter Åström/artist
Mikael Rundquist/artist and dramatist
Lennart Mörk/stage designer
Peter Dahl/artist
Thommy Berggren/actor and director

Thanks!
Eva-Maria Westberg, for continuous encouragement and fantastic patience.
Andreas von Gegerfeldt, for *many* long hot hours in the dark-room.
Naná de Graaff, for many long *hot* hours at the oven.
All you essay writers and artists, for wonderful and imaginative contributions.
Suzanne Houske-Andersson and Sue Heap for advice with the translation.

Colophon
The bodytext is set in Electra 10,5/12 pt, picture captions in News Gothic 7/8,5 pt.
The paper: insert Munken Book Cream 150 g, jacket Galerie Art 170 g.
Printing: Fälth & Hässler, Värnamo 2001